Fundació Joan Miró

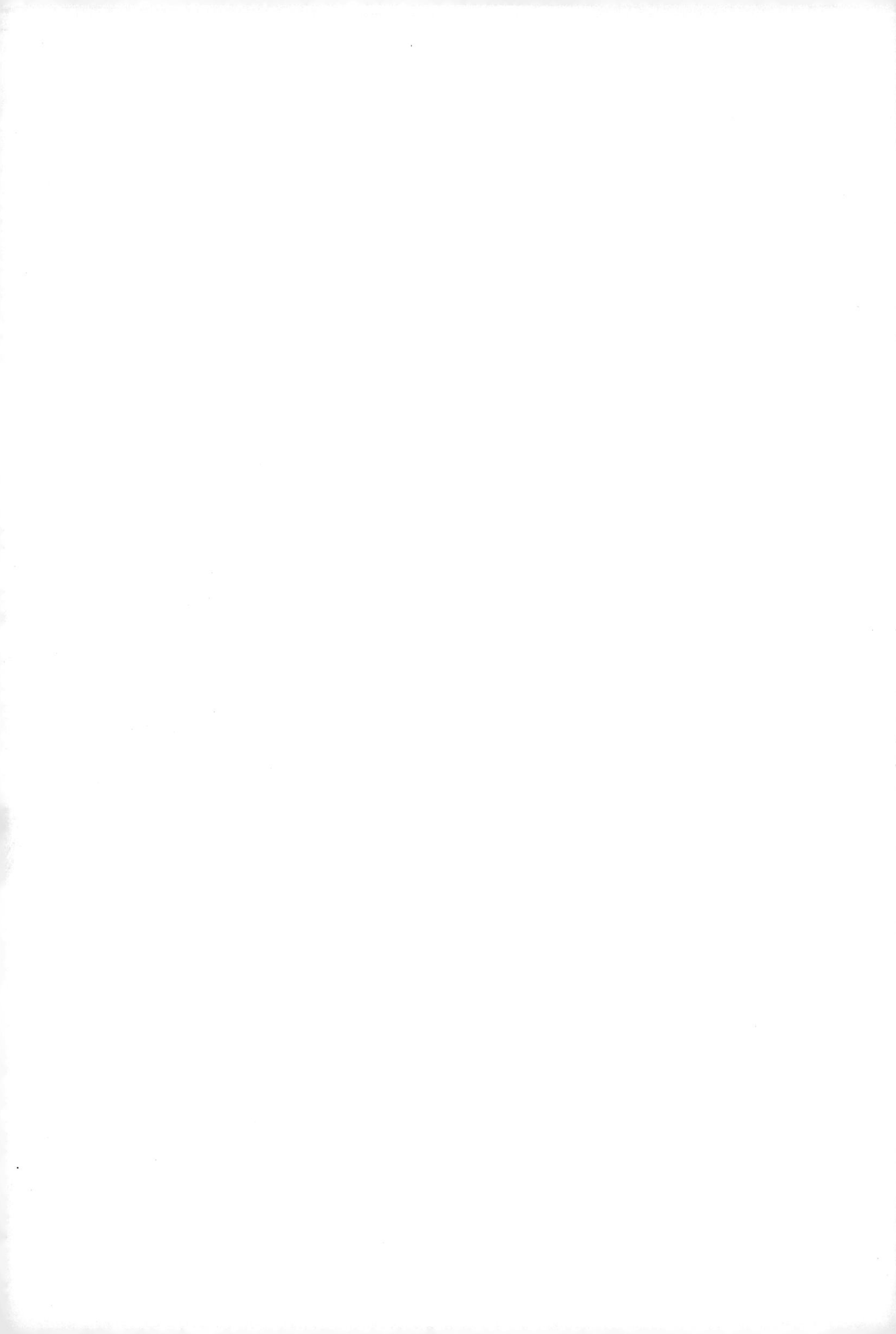

Fundació Joan Miró

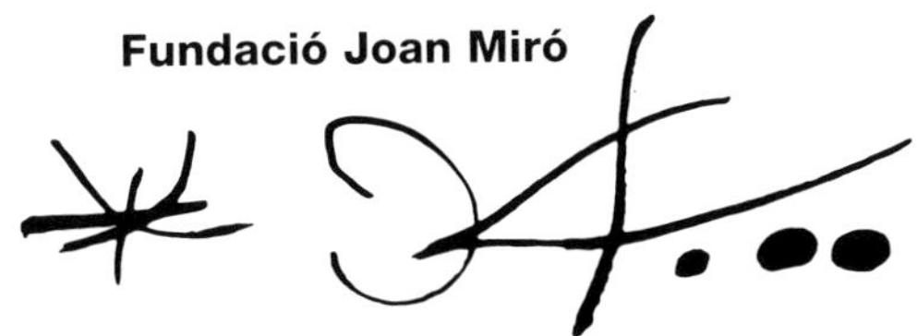

Fundació Joan Miró
Guidebook

Edited by Rosa Maria Malet

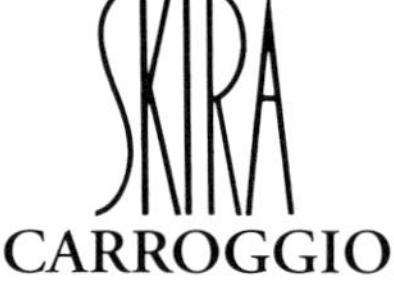

CARROGGIO

*Distributed in North America and Latin America by Abbeville Publishing Group, 22 Cortlandt St., New York, NY 10007, USA.
Distributed elsewhere in the world by Thames and Hudson Ltd., 181a High Holborn, London WC1V 7QX, United Kingdom.*

Cover illustration
Joan Miró: *Flame in space and naked woman*, 1932

Coordination
Victòria Izquierdo Brichs

Documentation
Carme Escudero

English translation
Joanna Martinez

Design
Marcello Francone

Maquette
Monica Temporiti

Photographs of Miró's works
Jaume Blassi

I.S.B.N.: 84-7254-764-7
D.L.: B-13.409-99
Printed in Spain

Contents

Joan Miró at the entrance to the Foundation

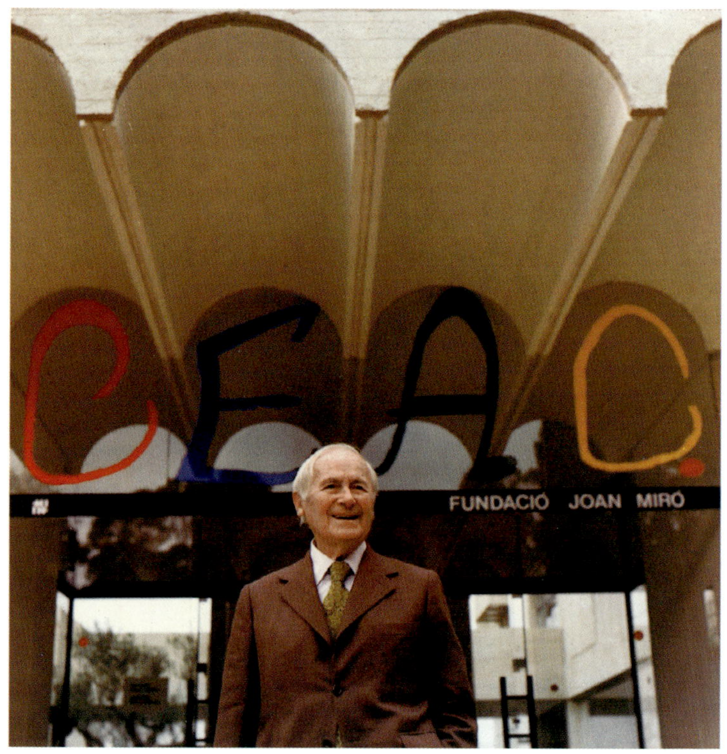

What is the Joan Miró Foundation?

Origins

The Joan Miró Foundation was the first public institution set up in Barcelona to focus entirely on contemporary art.

In 1968, the year of Joan Miró's seventy-fifth birthday, the City Council organised a large retrospective exhibition of his work at the Antic Hospital de la Santa Creu. The remarkable selection of works on show – some from museums and private collections and others from the artist's studio in Majorca – was proof of the interest in his oeuvre and of the importance of his contribution to the art of the twentieth century.

Realising that it would be relatively easy to make his work accessible to the public on a permanent basis, Miró, with the encouragement of his friend Joan Prats, decided to set up the Foundation. His intention was to create a dynamic centre where art experts and the public in general would come in contact not only with his own work but also with the main currents in twentieth-century art, and where support would also be provided for the creative talents of young artists.

The idea of a foundation, a form of institution with a long tradition in Catalonia, seemed to be the most suitable way of ensuring complete independence.

Josep Lluís Sert, a founder member of GATCPAC (Grup d'Arquitectes i Tècnics Catalans per al Progrés de l'Arquitectura Contemporània) and a friend of Joan Miró, drew up the plans for the building and supervised its construction. The City Council provided the land and paid for part of the construction costs.

The Building

Joan Miró and Josep Lluís Sert had first met in 1932, and became close friends in 1937 when they both worked on the Spanish Republican Government's pavilion at the Paris World Fair.

The pavilion, designed by Josep Lluís Sert and Luis Lacasa, contained among other pieces Picasso's *Guernica, Montserrat* by Julio González, the *Mercury fountain* by Alexander Calder and *The reaper* by Joan Miró. It was the first building by Sert designed specifically to house works of art, and was followed some years later by Miró's own studio in Majorca (1956), the Fondation Maeght at Saint-Paul-de-Vence (1964) and finally the Joan Miró Foundation in Barcelona (1975). In the Joan Miró Foundation, Sert created an open-plan structure where the interior space communicated with the exterior, producing a perfect balance between architecture and landscape.

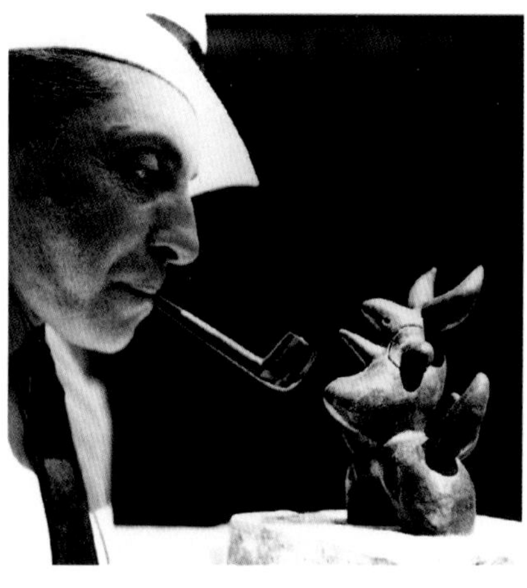

Joan Prats contemplating *the Moon bird*

From the outset, he gave considerable thought to resolving the two main difficulties affecting places in which works of art are exhibited: lighting and the way visitors circulate.

In order to make the maximum use of daylight, he decided to construct skylights in the form of quadrants through which reflected sunlight penetrates the building from above in such a way that no shadows are produced and no rays of light shine directly on to the works of art or into the eyes of visitors, whatever the height of the sun above the horizon according to the time of day or season of the year.

The circulation of visitors was organised around the central patio – the origin of which can be found in the impluvium of a Roman house and in medieval cloisters – so that the same point need not be passed more than once.

The basic material used is reinforced concrete, treated in such a way that the characteristic grey colour is replaced by the typical white of Mediterranean buildings. On the outside, the marks left by the shuttering are combined with prefabricated panels of a

The Joan Miró Foundation

The central patio and terrace

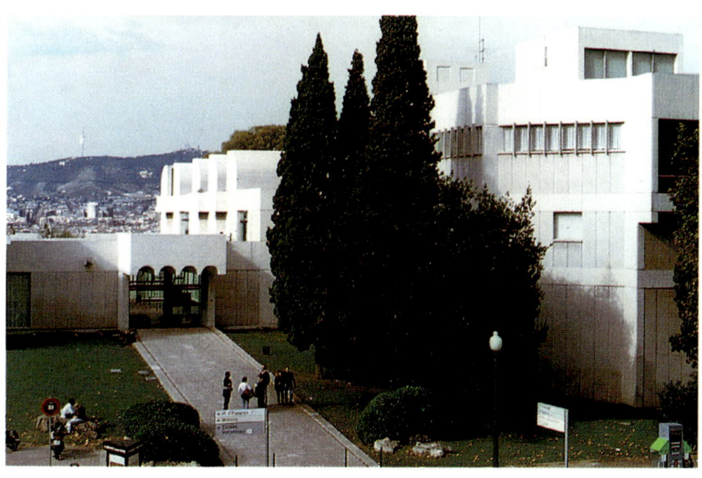

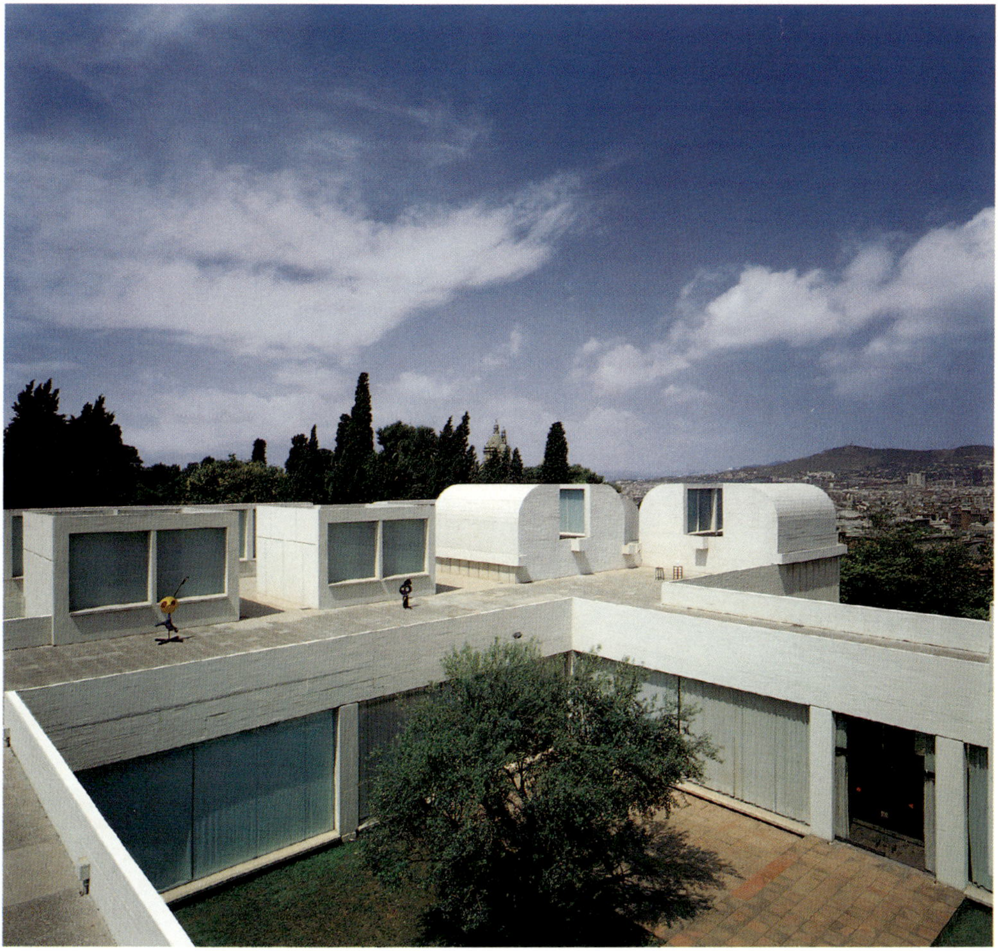

granular texture. The inside walls are whitewashed in typical local fashion, creating a restful atmosphere conducive to contemplation. The other materials used are also redolent of vernacular architecture in the Mediterranean: terracotta tiles, wooden edgings to the steps, etc. The plain yet pleasing forms of Sert's designs have the same origins: the central patio already mentioned, the apertures linking interior and exterior, and the shallow vaulted ceilings that create subtle tones of white and grey. One of the distinctive features of the outside of the building is the octagonal tower containing the Auditorium, the Library and the room housing the display of Miró's works on paper.

Ten years after the opening of the Foundation and two years after Miró's death, the Board of Trustees decided to enlarge Sert's original building due to the fact that the number of activities was increasing and that space was needed for a permanent exhibition of the works in the Foundation's collections.

The architect commissioned to carry out this important and delicate task was Jaume Freixa, a pupil of Sert's who had worked with him for many years at Harvard and had actively participated in the whole process of designing the Foundation.

Aware of the provisions for the future that Sert himself had made at a time when it would have been unrealistic to think there could ever be any need for enlargement, Freixa opted for an extension that clearly respected the existing building and did nothing to disrupt its uniformity.

Thus, in 1988, without altering the basic premises of Sert's architecture, the Foundation opened the new spaces designed by Jaume Freixa. In addition to increasing the size of the exhibition area by 45%, these provided room for a new Book Shop and for the Bar-Restaurant.

The Collections

The most important aspect of the Foundation's collections is without doubt its valuable stock of works by Joan Miró, consisting of over 10,000 items: 217 paintings, 178 sculptures, 9 textiles, the almost complete graphic works, and a collection of around 7,000 drawings, sketches and notes. Practically all these pieces were donated by Miró himself.

Alexander Calder: *Mercury fountain*, 1937

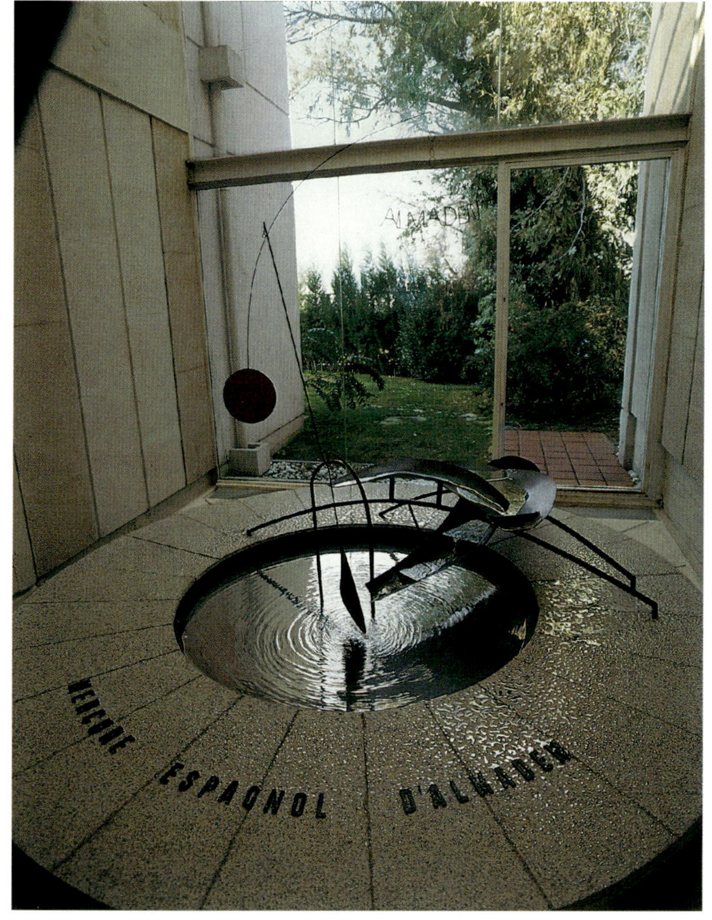

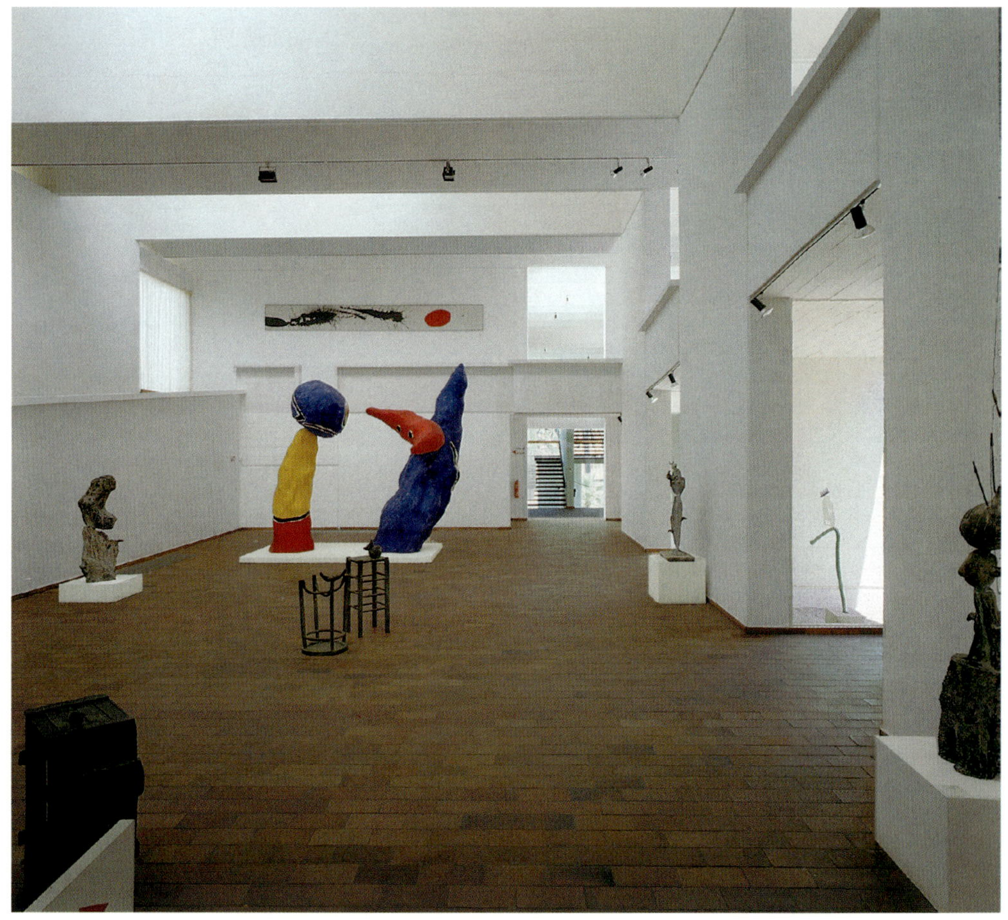

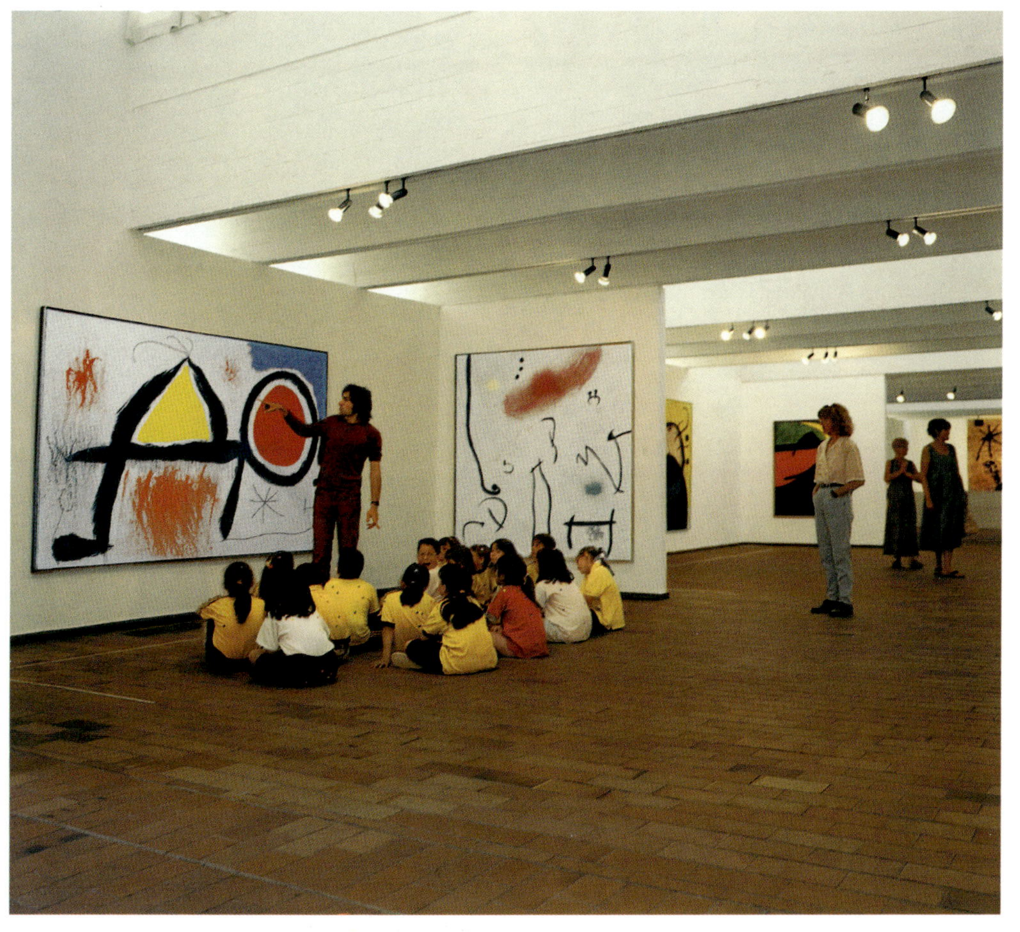

In addition, there are the works from her personal collection on permanent loan from Miró's wife, Pilar Juncosa de Miró. After her death, these passed to her heirs, but have continued on permanent loan to the Foundation in order to respect the founder's initial intentions. Consisting of a number of paintings from different periods, this collection gives a good overall view of the development of the artist's work.

The private collection of Miró's works assembled by Joan Prats, his close friend and the driving force behind the idea of setting up the Foundation, was donated at the outset and also shows the process of consolidation of the artist's pictorial language.

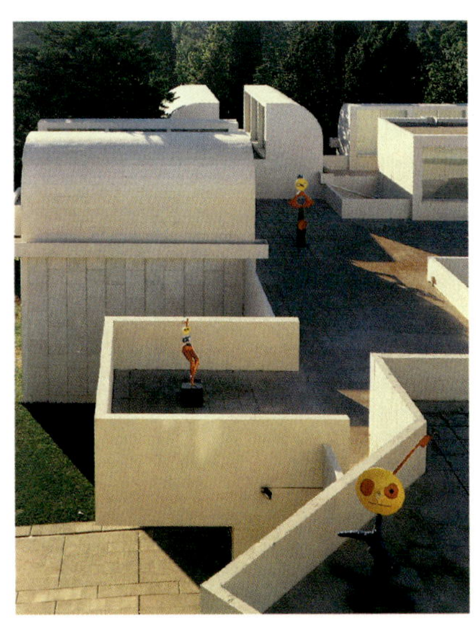

The roof terraces

The Foundation also holds works that Miró donated to Barcelona City Council with the stipulation that they should be kept at the Foundation after the closure of the 1968 exhibition at the Antic Hospital de la Santa Creu.

Further works by Miró have been donated to the Foundation by Marguerite and Aimé Maeght, Pierre Matisse, Manuel de Muga, David Fernández Miró, Josep Lluís Sert, Francesc Farreras, Josep Royo and Gérald Cramer.

The Foundation has a representative selection of the bronze sculptures produced by Miró between the mid-1940s and the late 1970s. It also has one object-sculpture dated 1946 and four from the 1950s, in addition to the maquettes of two of his later large-format sculptures: the monumental group for the district of La Défense in Paris (1975) and *Woman and bird* (1981-82) in the Parc de Joan Miró in Barcelona.

It was not until 1972 that Miró began to work with textiles. In the innovative spirit that characterises his entire oeuvre, and with the technical assistance of Josep Royo, he produced a number of pieces – *sobreteixims* and sacks – that although similar to tapestry cannot strictly speaking be classed as such. The Foundation has four examples of each type. The large *Tapestry of the Foundation*, dated 1979, clearly shows the artist's desire to transport colours and textures from a painted surface to one formed of warp and weft.

Although Miró's contacts with the theatre were sporadic, the very varied material in the Foundation connected with this facet of his work is eloquent proof of its importance.

Firstly, there is the entire collection of drawings, sketches and maquettes related to the world of ballet. From this we can see how closely Miró's work was linked to the movements of the dancers on stage when he designed the sets and costumes for *Jeux d'enfants,* performed by the Ballets Russes de Montecarlo in 1932.

Secondly, there are the figures used in the performance of *Mori el Merma,* which were created by the Teatre de la Claca group on the basis of the typical forms found in Miró's drawings and were painted by the artist himself. These show the effects of his work in conquering not only the third dimension but movement too.

Of Miró's extensive output of graphic works, the Foundation holds at least two copies of practically every one of the original prints, books and posters he produced. In some cases, in addition to the two copies – one in the archives and the other for display – the Foundation has all the proofs and maquettes where these have survived.

The graphic works held by the Foundation include one item that is unique in the world: the complete *Barcelona series.* Consisting of fifty lithographs in black and white, of which only five prints were pulled of each one, it was published as a result of the enthusiastic help of Joan Prats.

Nevertheless, the single factor that sets the Foundation apart from other museums containing a representative selection of the artist's work is unquestionably the total of almost 7,000 items that Alexandre Cirici named the "Miró papers" – the drawings, sketches and notes of various kinds made by Miró during the course of his life. It is thanks to this material that we can today follow the development of the artist's forms of expression, the concerns that led him always to explore new paths, his reflections on his own work, and so forth.

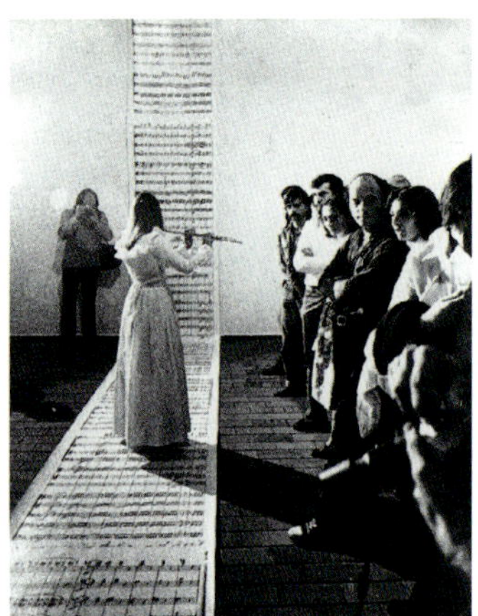

Recital by the Grup Instrumental Català, 1977

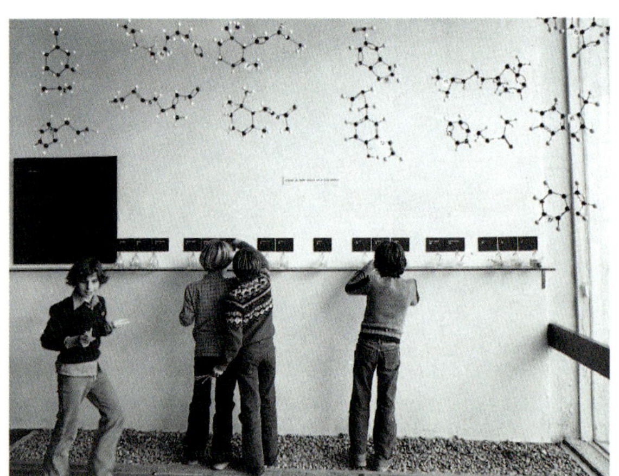

"Olfactory suggestions" exhibition, 1978

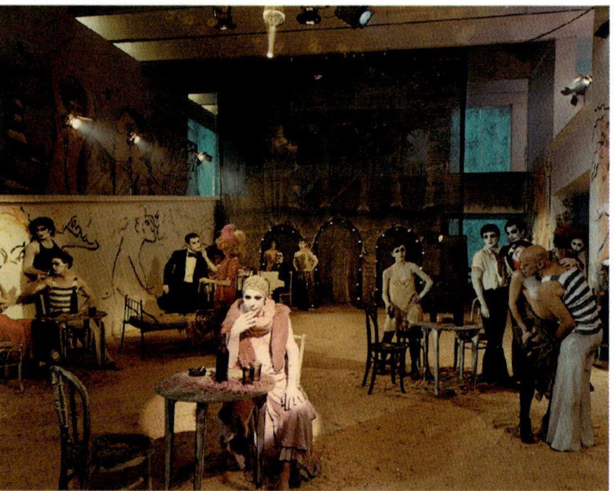

"Lindsay Kemp" exhibition, 1980

The Foundation, however, does not hold works of art only by Miró. It also has a small collection of contemporary pieces that was formed a year after his death through the generosity of artists, collectors and friends who wished to pay tribute to him.

This collection, consisting of donations and permanent loans, includes paintings, sculptures, photographs and objects by leading contemporaries of Miró such as Balthus, Bissier, Duchamp, Ernst, González, Lam, Llorens Artigas, Manolo, Man Ray, Masson, Matisse, Moore, Penn, Penrose, Tanguy and Torres-García, as well as works by later artists such as Adami, Alechinsky, Brossa, Català-Roca, Chillida, Guston, Motherwell, Newman, Rauschenberg, Saura and Tàpies.

Finally, the Foundation also holds a large collection of original prints by contemporary artists donated by Aimé Maeght in 1976, as well as other pieces contributed by Alfaro, Chillida and Villèlia, among others. An especially relevant place in this section is occupied by two works by Alexander Calder: *Corcovado,* donated by Josep Lluís Sert, and the *Mercury fountain,* originally designed for the Spanish Republican Government's pavilion at the 1937 Paris World Fair and donated to the Foundation by its creator as a token of his friendship with Miró.

Activities

The activities organised by the Foundation have generally been of two kinds, conditioned by its two separate but complementary focal points: the work of Joan Miró, and contemporary art in all its various manifestations.

Although Miró repeatedly expressed his wish that the Foundation should be a centre of living art and not merely a memorial to his own work, it is an undeniable fact that it possessed from the outset a highly exceptional asset in the shape of the works donated by the artist himself, which constitute the Foundation's permanent collection.

The Foundation has made this important collection accessible to the public through a constantly rotating selection of items on show, through loans to other institutions, and by organising exhibitions on different aspects of the founder's work, namely:

"Joan Miró: the twenties.
Mutation of reality", 1983

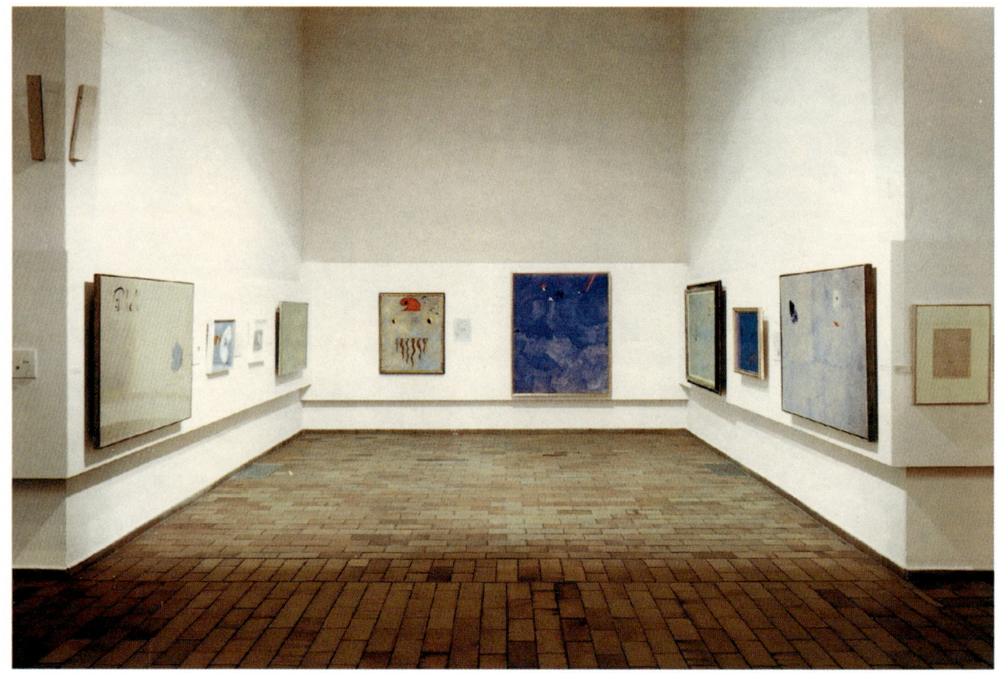

"Wolfgang Laib" exhibition, 1989

"Joan Miró 1983-1993" centenary exhibition

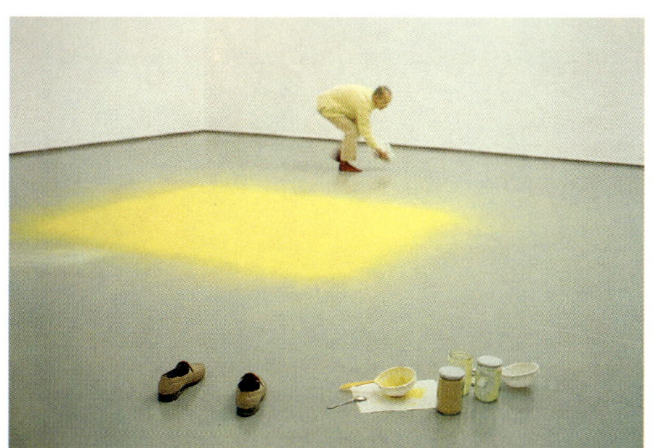

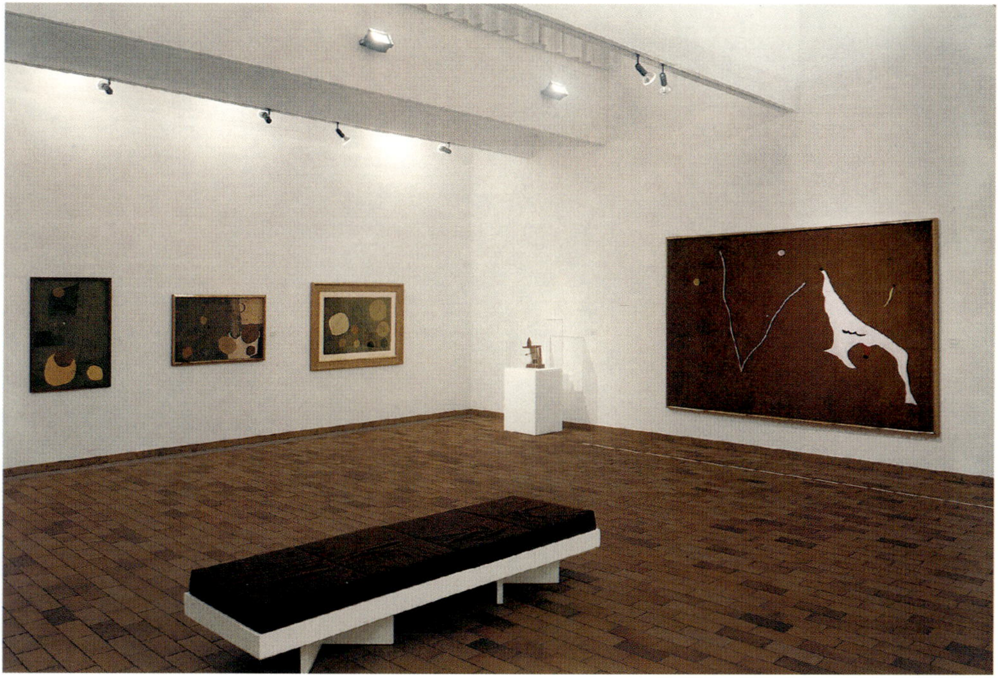

"Miró on stage", 1995

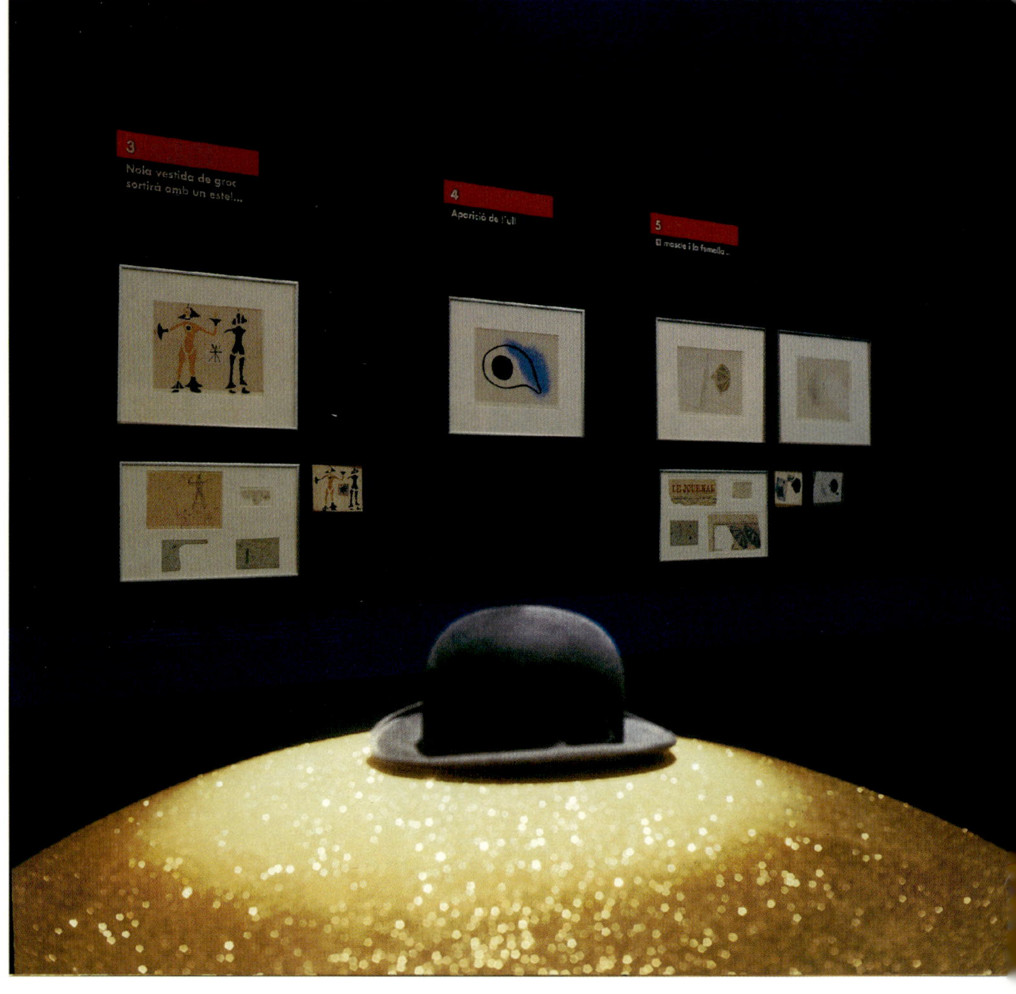

1976: 500 drawings by Joan Miró from the Foundation's collections
1980: Joan Miró: complete graphic works
1982: Joan Miró: painting, sculpture, ceramics, tapestry, theatre
1983: Joan Miró: the twenties. Mutation of reality
1985: Miró in close-up
1988: Impacts. Joan Miró: 1929-1941
1989: 109 books with Joan Miró
1993: Joan Miró: 1893-1993
1995: Miró on stage
1997: Joan Miró: equilibrium in space

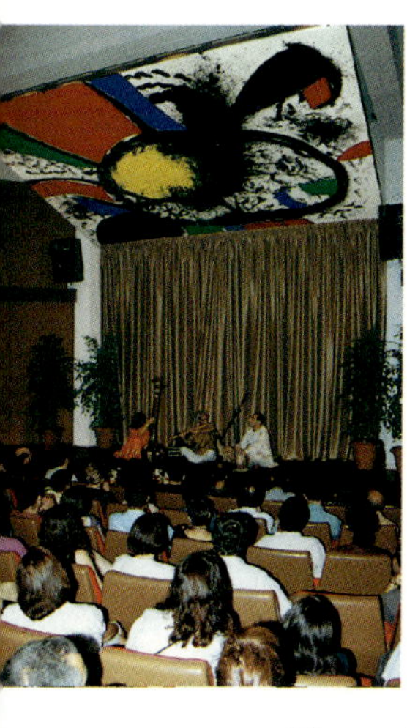

Recital in the Auditorium

When the idea of setting up the Joan Miró Foundation began to take shape in the early seventies, and even when it was finally opened to the public in 1975, the attention paid to contemporary art by official institutions was minimal.

To fill this gap, the Foundation began arranging a programme of temporary exhibitions parallel to its other activities. This programme was planned for the twofold purpose of making known to the public the leading names and movements in twentieth-century art and of publicising the work of younger artists.

The main temporary exhibitions have included:
1975: Tantric art
1976: Antoni Tàpies: works 1955-1976
1977: America, America (US painting 1945-1975)
1978: Olfactory suggestions
1979: The architecture of Josep Lluís Sert
1980: Antonio Saura: retrospective
1981: Henry Moore: sculptures, drawings and prints
1982: The principle of collage
1983: Kurt Schwitters
1984: Marcel Duchamp
1985: Russian avant-garde, 1910-1930
1986: Chillida: sculptures

"Andy Warhol" exhibition, 1996

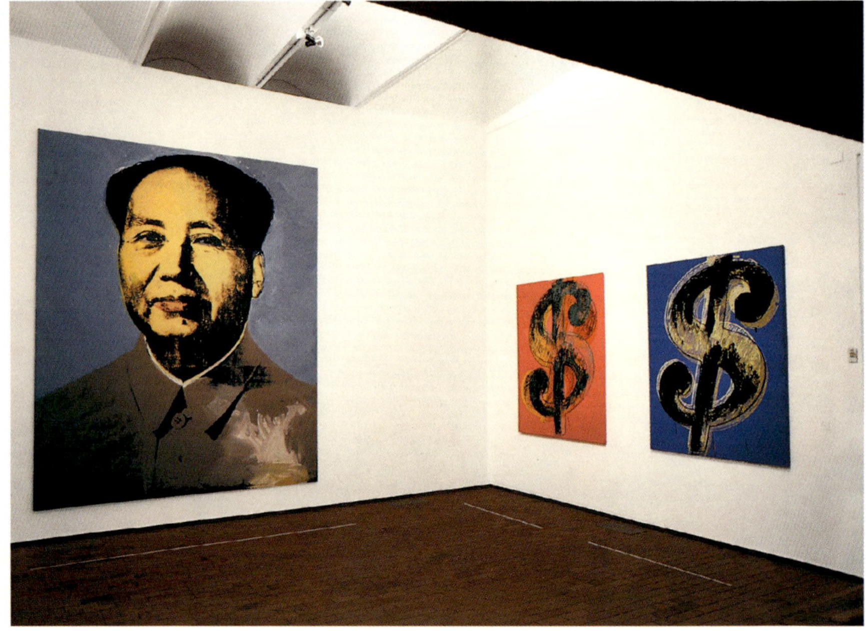

1987: The Giacomettis
1988: Donald Judd: sculpture 1965-1987
1989: 1st Joan Miró Drawing Triennial
1990: Joseph Beuys
1991: Antiquity/Modernity in twentieth-century art
1992: Moving image: Electronic art
1993: Wifredo Lam
1994: Mapplethorpe
1995: China: art of living, art of surviving
1996: Andy Warhol
1997: Alexander Calder
1998: René Magritte

During the first dozen years of the Foundation's existence, the experimental work of younger artists had its own particular venue in the "Espai 10" and later, after the extension was added, in the "Espai 13".

The Foundation's activities, however, extend beyond exhibitions and embrace very diverse sectors of the present cultural scene. Lectures, seminars and panel discussions are regularly held in conjunction with exhibitions. Other events include recitals of contemporary music, film shows, theatrical performances and, occasionally, performances by contemporary dance groups.

The Foundation also organises regular activities for children. It makes a special point of arranging guided tours of the permanent and temporary exhibitions, so that learning about art is treated as a complementary part of the academic programme. Younger visitors can also enjoy the theatrical performances for children held every weekend during term-time.

The Foundation's aim is to make visits by the public as pleasant as possible, not only through the interesting content of its programmes but also through the quality of the facilities available. Visitors are therefore allowed access to the Library specialising in contemporary art, which was initially based on the books donated by Miró but has continued to grow ever since.

The Book Shop and Gift Shop offer a wide selection of the latest books on contemporary art as well as reproductions, designer articles, and other goods.

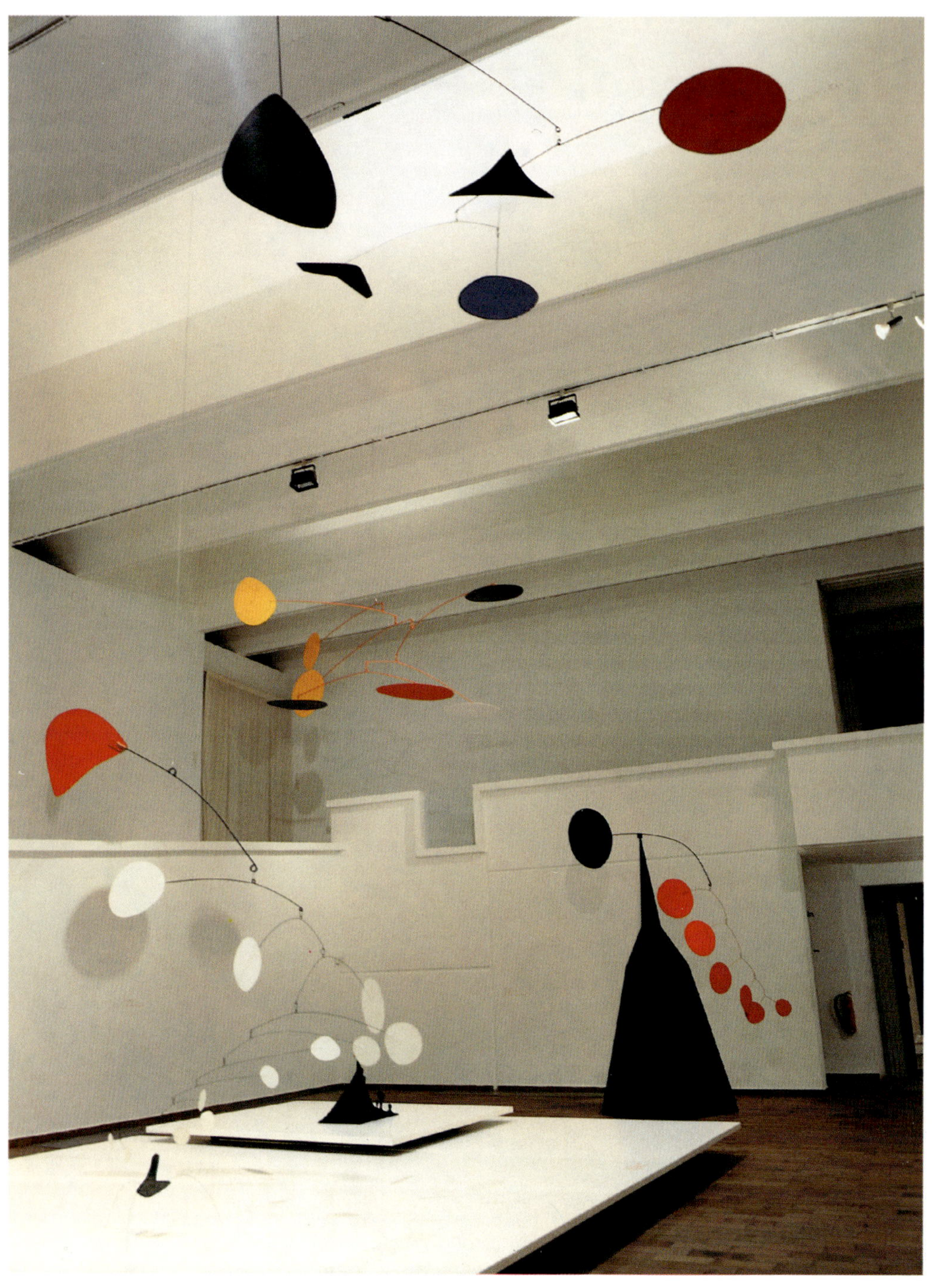

"Calder" exhibition, 1997

The Bar-Restaurant is just one more of the services provided by the Foundation for its visitors, where they can relax indoors or outdoors.

The Association of Friends of the Joan Miró Foundation offers a number of advantages, special concessions and activities to those who wish to support the institution set up by Miró.

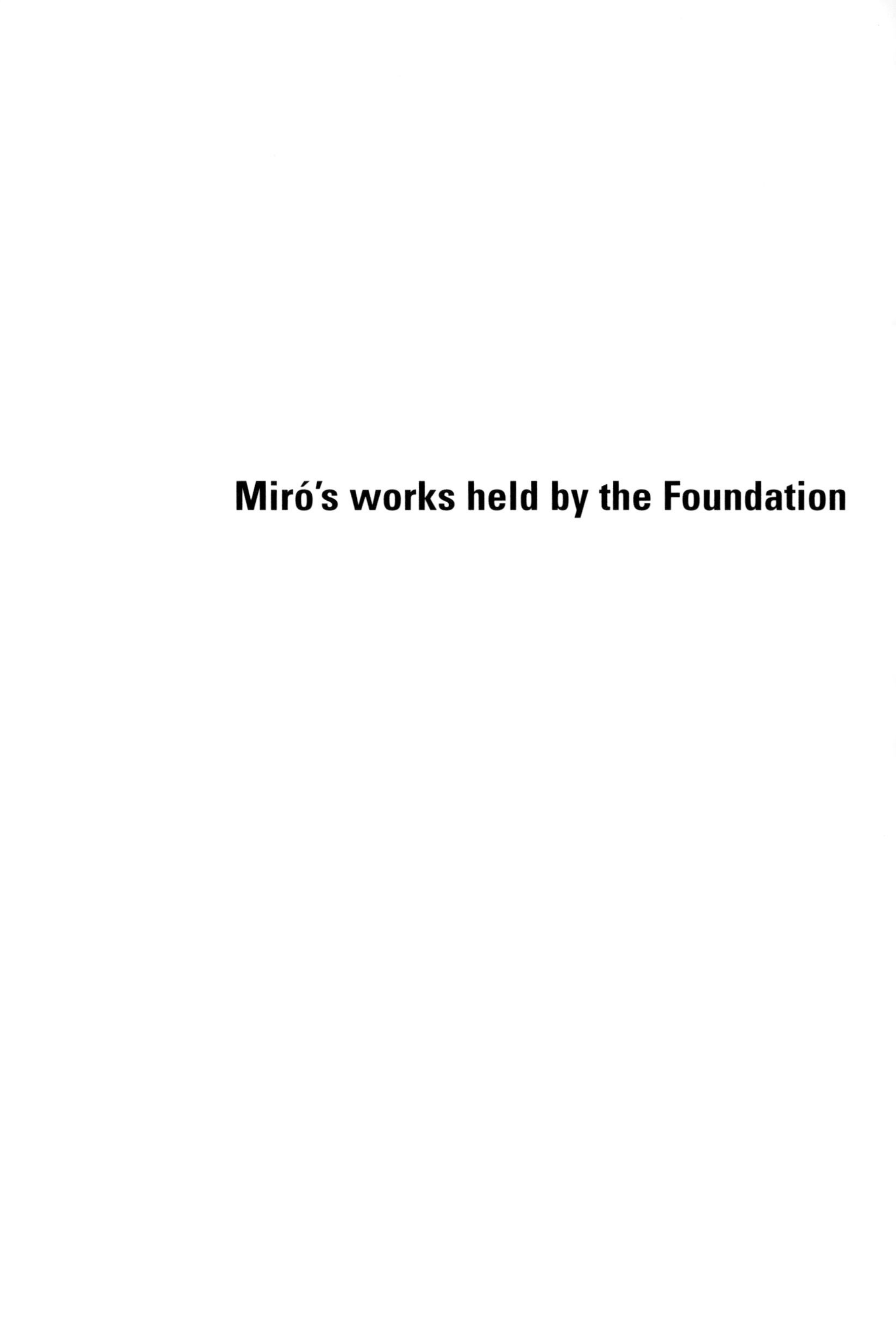

Miró's works held by the Foundation

The chiropodist, 1901

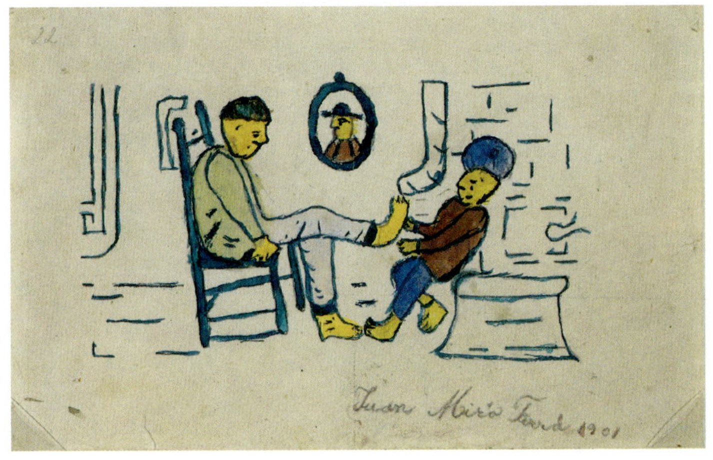

Early Drawings

The earliest reference to Miró's artistic activity comes from the collection of drawings held by the Foundation. This material is a valuable testimony that graphically describes the development of Miró's art, but it also allows us to follow the events and activities connected with his work.

The oldest of these drawings date back to 1901, when Miró was eight years old. They are very simple compositions, always in colour and generally portraying a single object – an umbrella, a flower pot, a tortoise. Among them, one piece stands out on account of its bright tones and the somewhat curious scene depicted: *The chiropodist.* This drawing is almost a prediction of the importance that Miró was subsequently to attach to the foot. According to him, this part of the human body keeps us in contact with the creative force emanating from the earth, and in his pictures it was later to be magnified by distorting its proportions, insinuated by means of an imprint, or sublimated by altering its meaning.

It was probably at school, in 1905, that Miró produced a series of drawings of a markedly romantic nature, a style inherited from the previous century that was very popular in conventional circles. The dominant themes of these pieces are rural landscapes or imaginary medieval scenes.

Contrasting with these drawings, probably done as copying exercises at school, is a sketchbook from the summer of the following year. During the long summer holidays, Miró used to

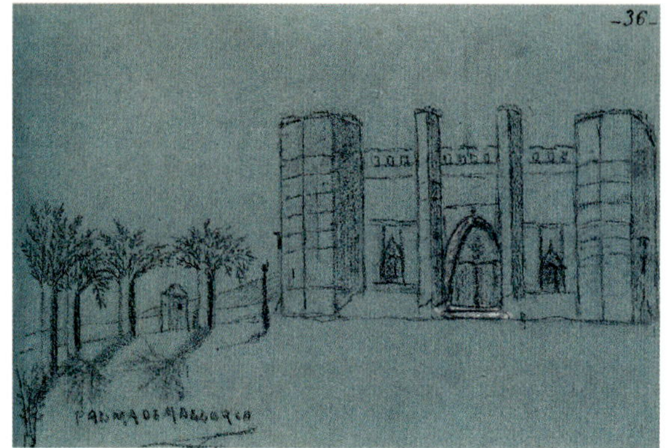

Palma de Mallorca. The Llotja, c. 1906

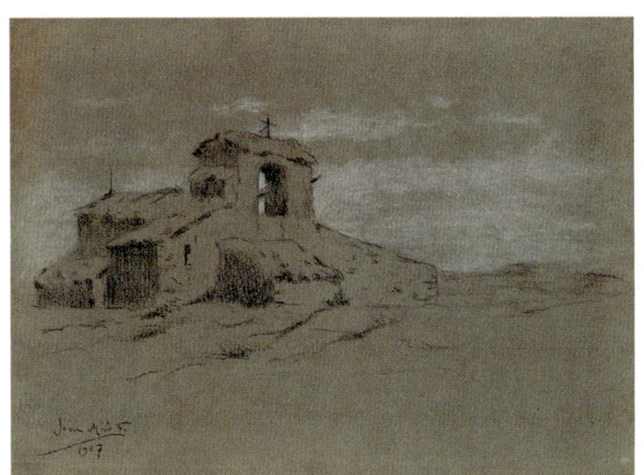

Chapel, 1907

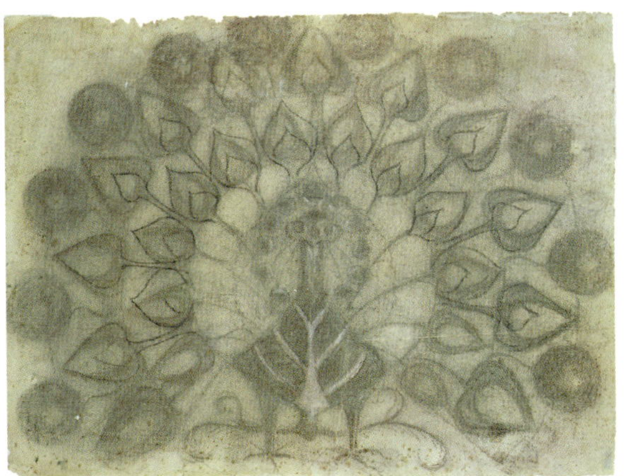

Peacock, c. 1908

Snake, c. 1908

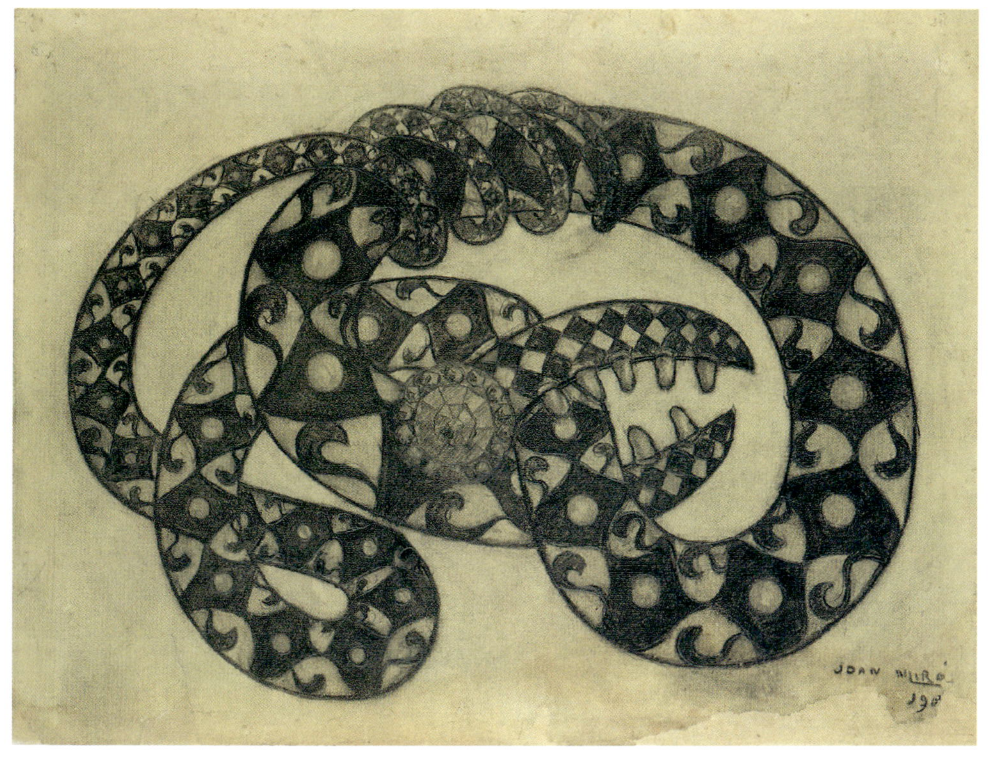

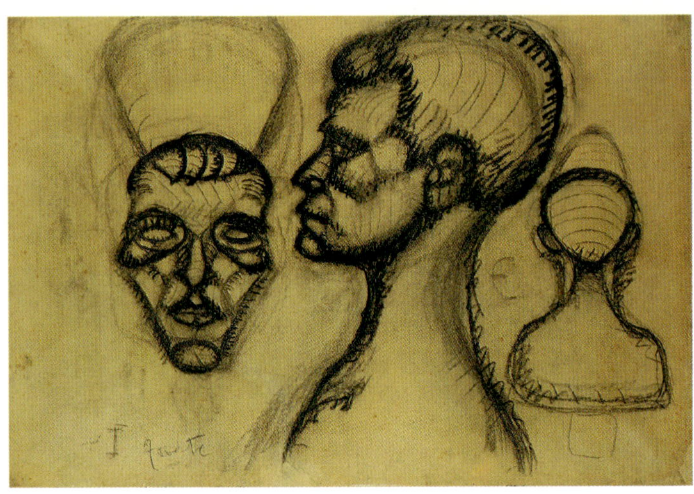

Exercise in touch. Three heads, c. 1912

spend time both at his paternal grandparents' house in Cornudella, and in Majorca where his maternal grandparents lived. The drawings of Prades, Siurana, Porrera and Cornudella bear witness to his holidays in the province of Tarragona, while in Majorca he drew the typical windmills, Bellver Castle, and the port and Llotja (exchange) in Palma.

After finishing primary school in 1907, Miró enrolled in the Escola de Comerç in Barcelona and also in the Llotja school of art. There he combined his commercial studies, undertaken on his father's orders, with his incipient artistic vocation. Although he always rejected anything that did not involve live creation and hated academicism and convention, he always had fond memories of his time at the Llotja, especially his relationship with two teachers, Modest Urgell (1839-1919) and Josep Pascó (1855-1910).

The Foundation holds a good number of drawings done by Miró in Modest Urgell's classes. The subjects represented – landscapes with cemeteries, crumbling walls, cypress trees, etc. – show clearly the influence of the master that was to be evident throughout his oeuvre. From Modest Urgell he acquired a taste for empty spaces, for the line of the horizon defining the earth and sky, and for the constant presence of heavenly bodies. References to Urgell became almost an obsession in the final months of Miró's life and confirm the high regard in which he held him as a teacher.

The only records of Josep Pascó's classes are two exceptional drawings, one of a peacock and the other of a snake. In the ornamental style and curvaceous lines of both pieces, which were possibly to be used as designs for jewellery, the influence of the Art Nouveau of the time can be clearly felt.

The panorama of Miró's formative years is completed by the drawings from the period when he attended classes at the art school run by Francesc Galí (1880-1965), a private academy that was more open-minded than the Llotja. The teaching there was not limited to traditional classes on the school premises, but often included sessions spent sketching in the open air, music recitals, poetry readings and debates.

To this period can be dated several curious drawings produced not by viewing the subject but by perceiving it through touch. For the first time, a human figure appears – or part of one, in this case, for the drawings are different studies of heads.

Francesc Galí imposed this particular exercise on his pupil after noting his extraordinary gifts as a colourist but his difficulty in reproducing form. By letting the sense of touch take over, Galí unwittingly provided Miró with a new perspective that he was not to explore in depth until later: the possibility of working in three dimensions.

Mas d'en Poca, 1914

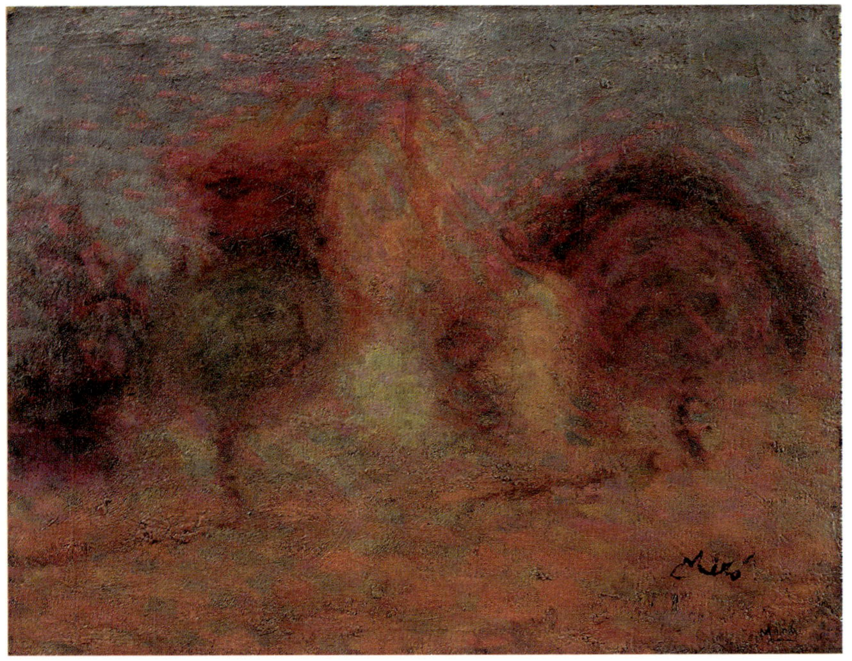

Barcelona / Mont-roig

The first catalogued paintings by Joan Miró date from 1914. In them we again find the subjects that appeared so often in his drawings, especially landscape. One notable work from this period is *Mas d'en Poca,* a representational painting in exuberant colours.

In order to perfect his drawing techniques, Miró left Galí's school in 1915 and joined the Cercle Artístic de Sant Lluc, where he attended lessons in life-drawing until he left for Paris.

Preserved from his days at the Cercle Artístic are three loose drawings and three sketchbooks containing mainly male and female nudes. Produced with very limited materials – paper and graphite pencil or ink – they allow us to follow the artist's development, concerned at times with capturing a gesture and at others with depicting the precise features of a face or transmitting movement in a rapid stroke.

Aside from their documentary value, these sketchbooks reveal some of Miró's interests at the time, since in addition to the models we find the dancers, clowns and music-hall figures that enlivened Barcelona's night-life and that Miró discovered in the company of Sebastià Gasch. Of particular note among the drawings from this period held at the Foundation is *Female nude,* from the Prats collection.

Once again we find a landscape – a subject that Miró never abandoned – though this time with a certain post-Impressionist influence, in *Beach at Mont-roig,* 1916.

Female nude, 1915

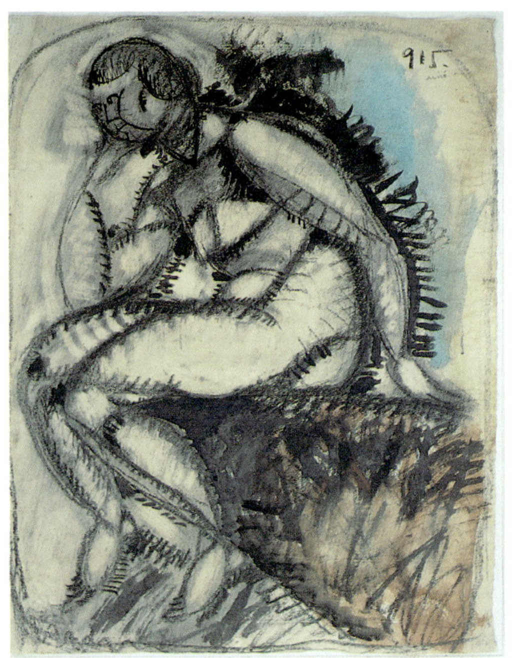

Female nude, 1917. Gift of Joan Prats

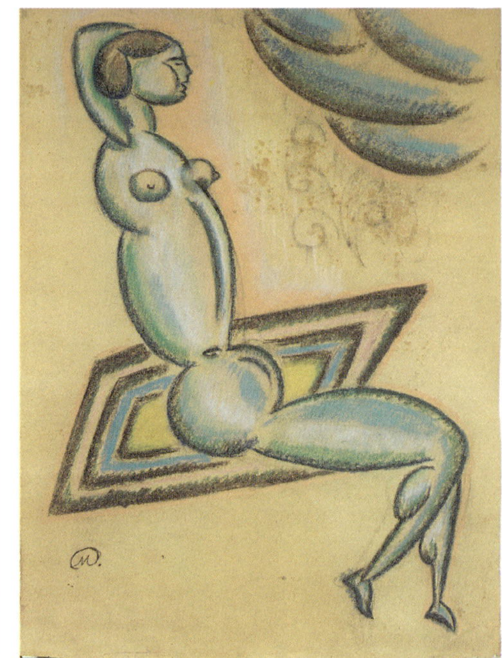

Beach at Mont-roig, 1916

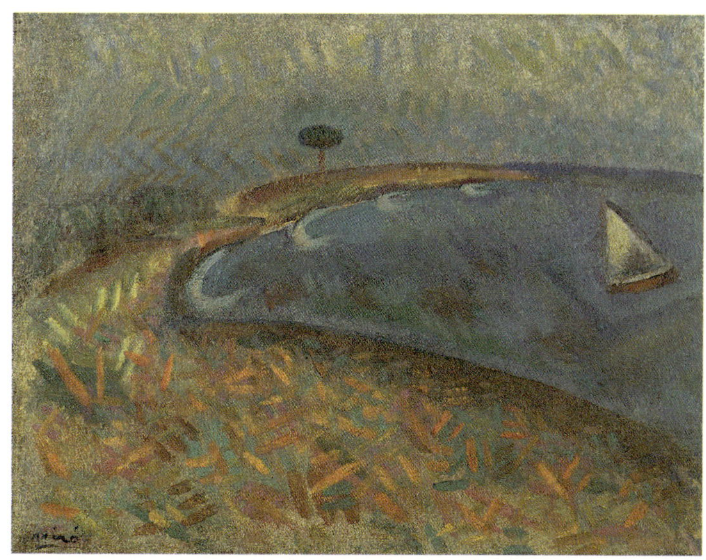

Chapel of Sant Joan d'Horta, 1917. Gift of Joan Prats

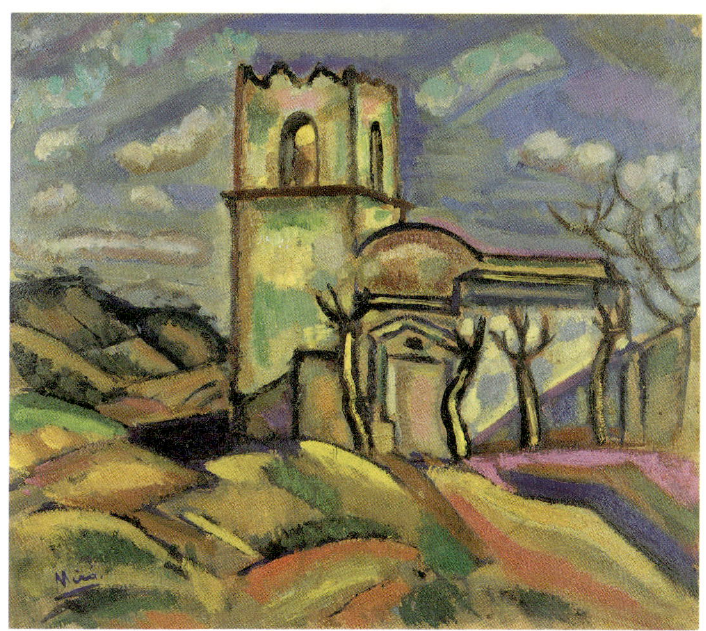

Street in Pedralbes, 1917. Gift of
Joan Prats

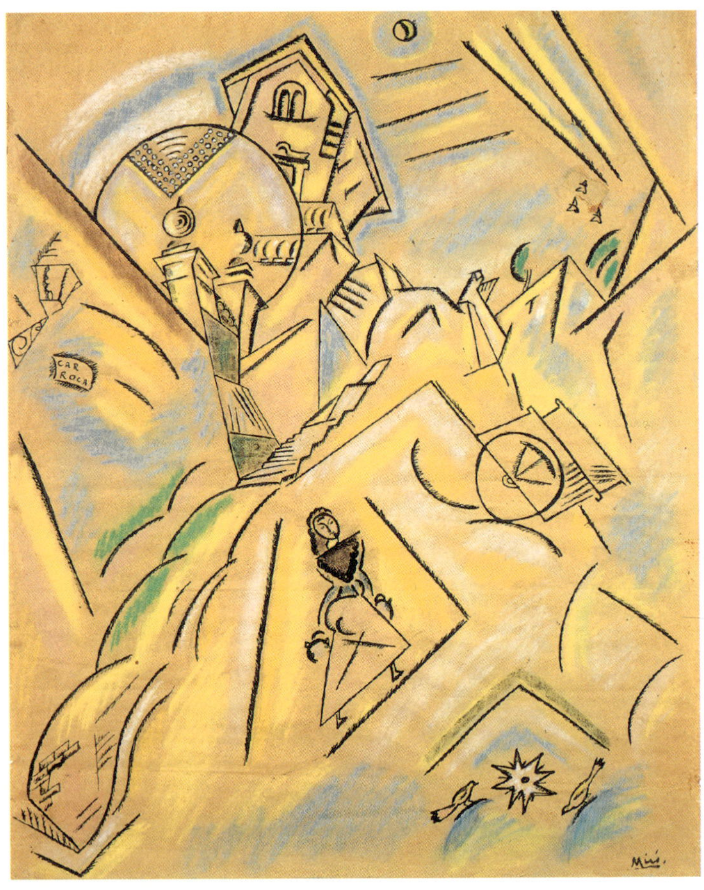

In 1917, artistic and intellectual life in Barcelona experienced a brief but intense period of effervescence with the arrival of artists and intellectuals fleeing from the scene of the First World War. Among them was Francis Picabia, a strong stimulus for those who wanted to keep abreast of the latest developments in avant-garde art. It was thanks to him that the Dada movement reached Barcelona, where he began publication of the review *391.*

Miró was not indifferent to these events, though he took a passive rather than active part in them. His style had yet to be defined and his artistic persona was as yet unformed when Dada made its impact on the city.

His work at that time was basically influenced by Fauvism on the one hand, and by Cubism and even more so by Cézanne on the other. Thus, the rich and in many cases unrealistic colours, the thick brush strokes and a discreet distortion of forms – the principal features of Fauvism – can be seen in *Chapel of Sant Joan d'Horta.* The alteration of the classical values of painting brought about by the Cubist concept of space is timidly reflected in *Street in Pedralbes.*

Except for the paintings, most of which are now in private collections and foreign museums, the works by Miró that have survived from the period between his leaving the Cercle Artístic de Sant Lluc and 1923 are not many in number. Nevertheless, we know that during those years certain events took place that were of major importance to the artist and to the development of his work.

In 1918, the Barcelona gallery owner Josep Dalmau organised Miró's first solo exhibition, which contained most of the canvases painted between 1914 and 1917: landscapes, still-lifes and portraits.

After passing the test of showing his work outside his studio, Miró, now fully freed from the Fauve influence, embarked on a slowly and meticulously executed style of painting, and in the following year produced *Portrait of a young girl.*

In March 1920, he visited Paris for the first time, but did not move there until 1921. He took up residence in number 45 Rue Blomet, in the studio used in the summers by the sculptor Pablo

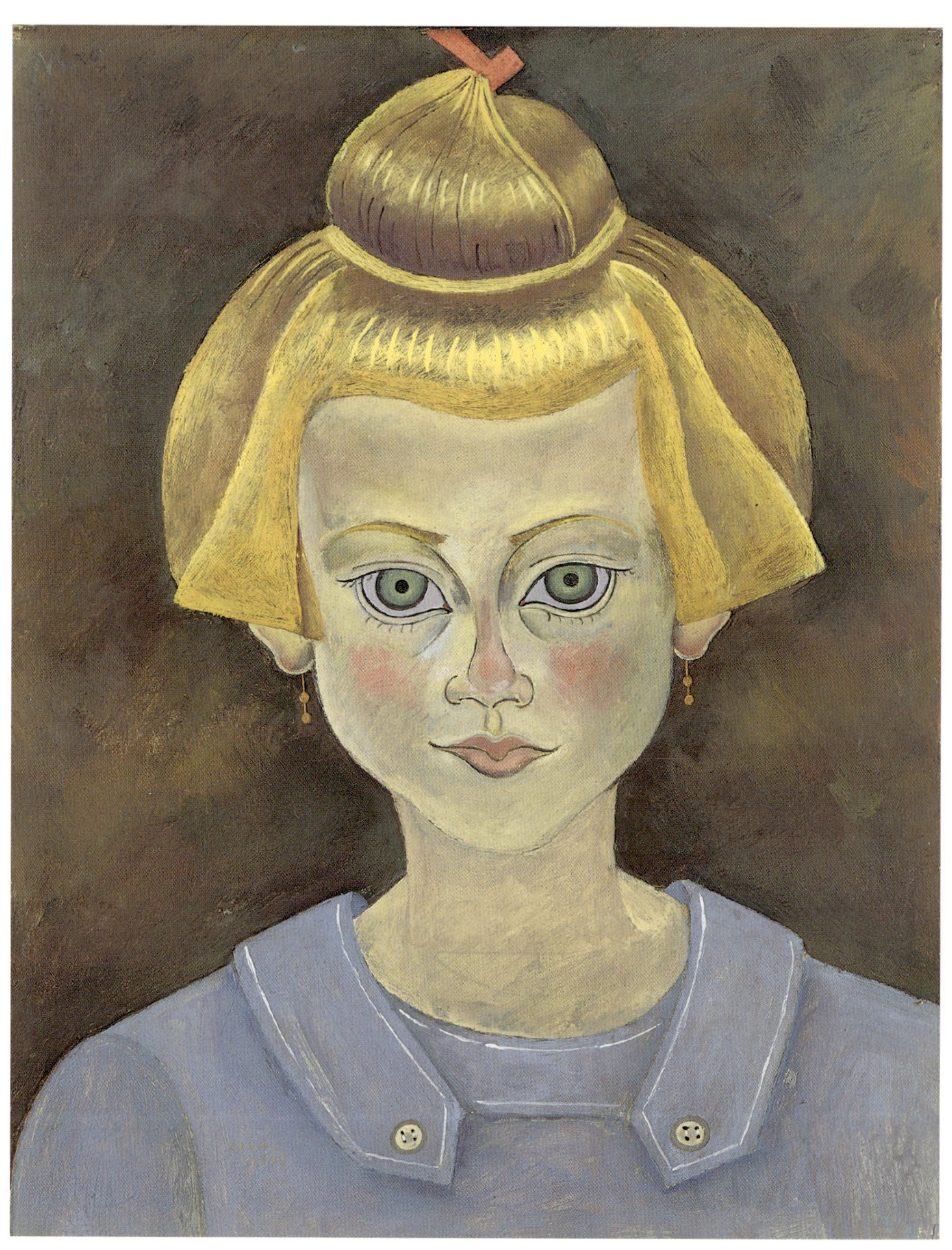

Portrait of a young girl, 1919.
Gift of Joan Prats

Gargallo, a teacher at the Escola de Belles Arts in Barcelona, but empty during the rest of the academic year.

In Paris, Miró continued painting in the minutely detailed style that had defined his work during the years immediately before leaving Spain and that he was to keep up until 1922, when he finished painting *The farm.* This masterpiece from his *détailliste* period is a milestone in Miró's career, for it contains the germs of his subsequent output: his love of the stars, respect for agricultural work, fascination with everyday objects, interest in insects, pets and farm animals, etc.

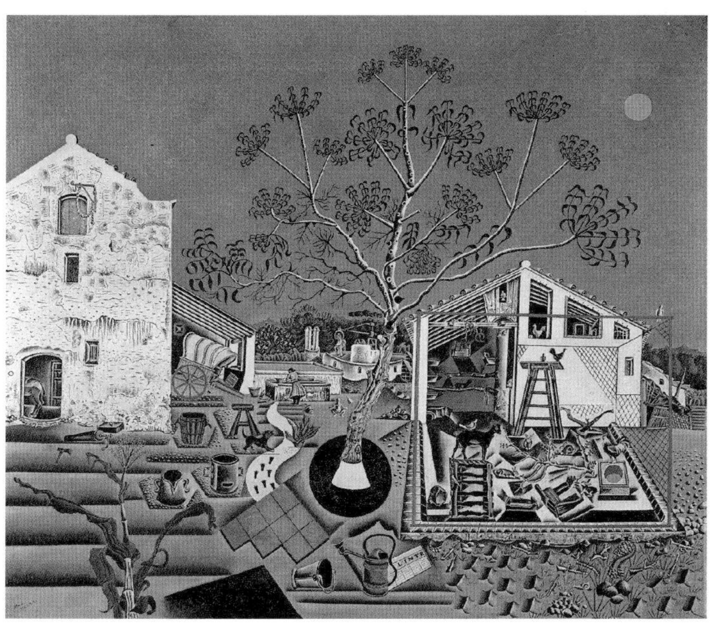

The farm, 1921-22. National Gallery of Art, Washington. Mary Hemingway Bequest

The wine bottle, 1924.
On permanent loan from Dolors
Fernández

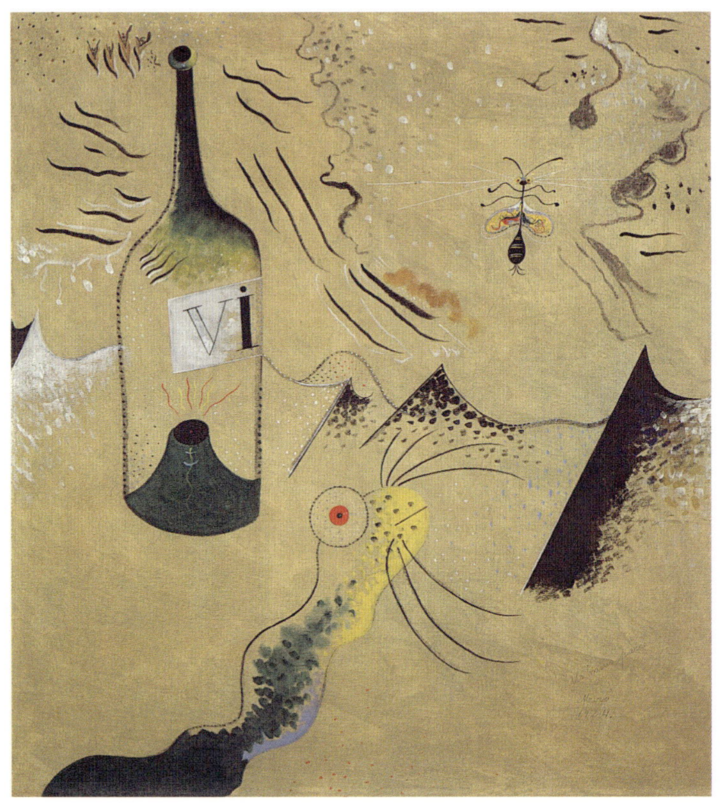

Paris

In the middle of 1924, Miró returned to Paris having spent the summer in Mont-roig, where he had started *Tilled field* and *Catalan landscape (The hunter).* His forms of expression as regards figurative representation were exhausted and he looked for new ways of transmitting his experiences through painting. These he found by distancing himself from his immediate surroundings. This restlessness coincided with the period of intellectual ferment in Paris, resulting in the first Surrealist Manifesto, published on 15th October that year.

Gradually realism gave way to suggestion and poetry in Miró's art. Form underwent a notable change as a consequence of a different approach. Instead of reproducing reality as his eyes perceived it, he let himself be invaded by what he saw and then processed it in a very subjective manner. Later on, in the studio, he painted what his feelings dictated as a consequence of the impact received.

During that time, drawing acquired a new dimension in the context of Miró's work, ceasing to be an end in itself and becoming instead a means to an end. Virtually all his sketches produced during the 1920s, and now at the Foundation, are a preliminary phase in the production of the final paintings. They enable us to compile a more than usually accurate inventory of his output during this decade, and to follow the process that preceded the execution of each painting from the moment

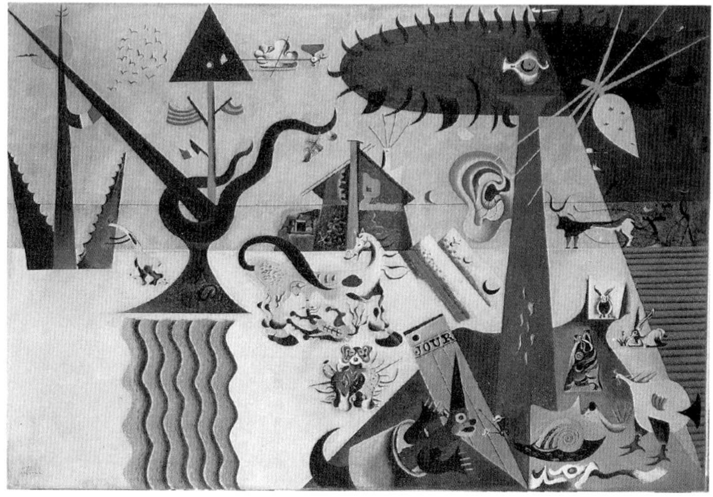

Tilled field, 1923-24. Solomon R. Guggenheim Museum, New York

when, still using reality as a point of reference, Miró ceased to portray it as an immediate experience.

This change in his approach heralded in *Tilled field* (1923-24) and consolidated in *Catalan landscape (The hunter)* (1923-24) – the preliminary sketches for which are preserved at the Foundation – can also be seen in *The wine bottle* (1924). In this small-format canvas, with its seemingly banal iconography and the inscription "To my parents" alongside the signature and date, Miró transmits a sense of vitality and of interchange between the celestial and the earthly creatures.

The possibility of following the creative process of Miró's paintings from this period, in which he faithfully followed his preliminary sketches, enables us to see very clearly his desire to refine and pare down forms in order to arrive at their essence. Furthermore, the very existence of these sketches indicates how far removed his work was from the Automatism propounded by the Surrealists.

Despite their different approaches, however, there was a certain similarity: while the Surrealist writers and artists based their explorations on the infinite possibilities offered by the world of dreams, Miró did not paint dreams but, by suggestion, provided the necessary elements to make the viewer dream.

On a monochrome ground – generally blue, ochre or brown – Miró placed weightless, indecipherable forms in perfect

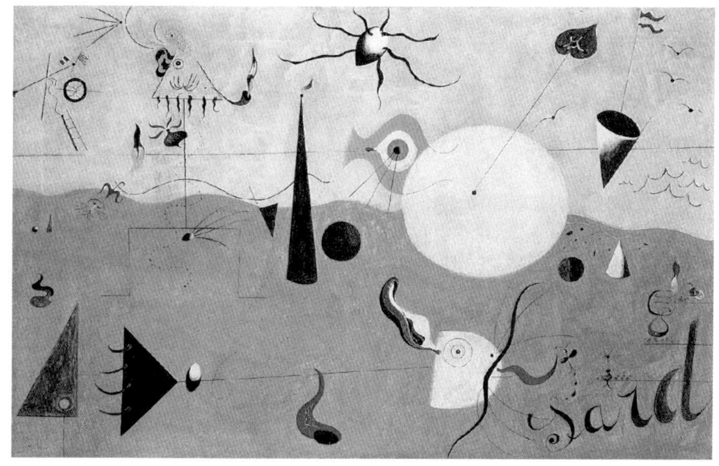

Catalan landscape (The hunter), 1923-24. The Museum of Modern Art, New York

equilibrium with the empty spaces, such as can be seen in *Painting* (1925) and *Painting* (1927). At other times – as in the case of *Painting (The white glove)* (1925) and *The music-hall usher* (1925) – the object or figure on the monochrome ground, taken from real life, transmutes reality into poetry. This was a determining factor in Miró's work of the 1920s.

It was also during this decade, in 1927, that Miró produced his first book illustration, for *Gertrudis* by the Catalan poet J. V. Foix, a close friend of his. This was the start of one of the most interesting ventures in Miró's artistic career – working together with his poet and writer friends on a considerable number of special limited editions.

In the spring of 1928, Miró went to Belgium and the Netherlands, where he visited the main cities and museums. The result of this trip was the series of *Dutch interiors.*

The genre paintings of the seventeenth-century Dutch masters made a deep impression on Miró. He bought postcards of a number of pictures and used these as the basis for reworking the compositions, subjecting the figures and objects to a form of metamorphosis. The Foundation's collections enable us to follow, for example, the entire process of production of *Dutch interior II* through the set of preliminary sketches based on the postcard of *The cat's dancing lesson* by Jan Steen (1626-1679).

Preliminary sketch for *Ceci est la couleur de mes rêves*, 1925

Preliminary sketch for *Stars in snails' genitals*, 1925

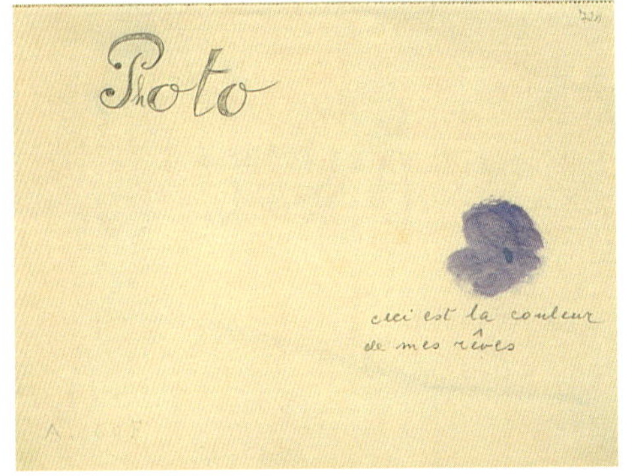

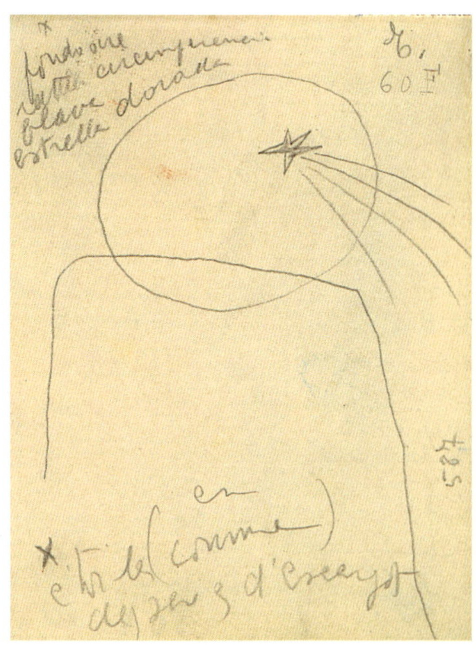

Painting, 1927.
Gift of Manuel de Muga

Painting, 1925.
Gift of Joan Prats

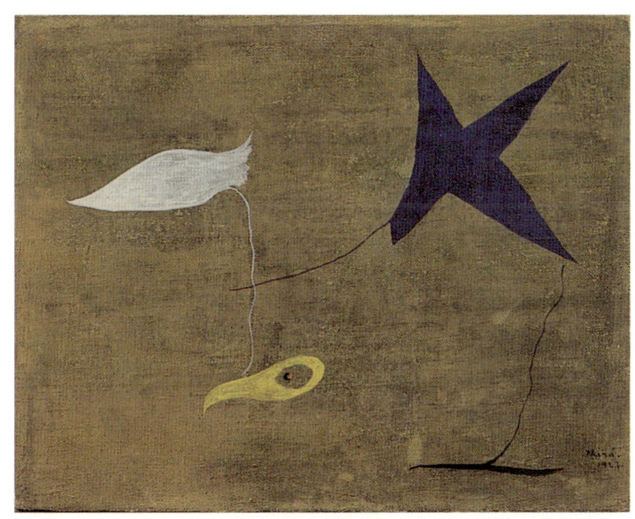

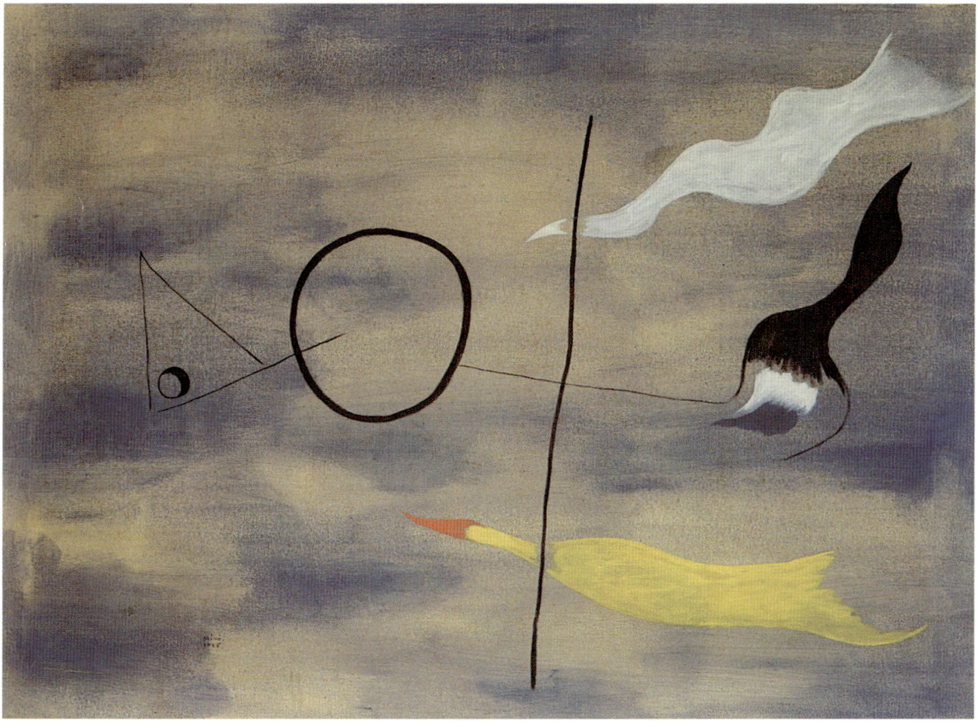

Similar approaches can be found in the series of four *Imaginary portraits*, dated 1929. On this occasion, Miró used as the starting point the *Portrait of Mrs. Mills in 1750* by George Engleheart (1752-1829), *Portrait of a lady in 1820* by Constable (1776-1837), *La Fornarina* by Raphael (1483-1520) and, finally, an advertisement for a machine cut out from a newspaper for the *Portrait of Queen Louise of Prussia*.

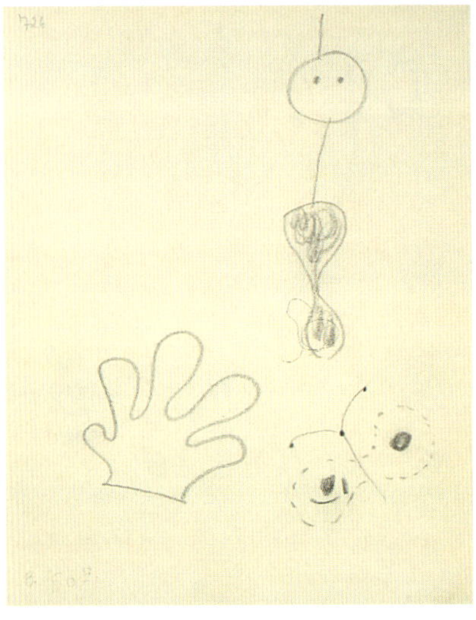

Preliminary sketch for *Painting (The white glove)*, 1925

The fact of taking the work of another artist – or, in the case of *Portrait of Queen Louise of Prussia,* simply a ready-made shape – as a reference point allowed Miró to analyse the pure form, stripping it down until he eventually produced a typically Mironian figure. This new approach required some effort, since he had to replace spontaneous creation with a painstaking process of maximum refinement. The series of preliminary sketches and notes bear witness to this.

By the late 1920s, this desire to get to the essence of things led Miró to eliminate everything he considered unnecessary and, as Michel Leiris has pointed out, to come close to the Zen aesthetic. *Untitled (Tree in the wind)* (1929) is not so very far removed from the style of oriental paintings in which the composition is determined by a single line and the different tones of black ink.

But soon Miró again felt the need to give a new focus to his work and to search for new forms of expression. The 1930s, which at the start seemed to be a period of crisis in his painting, turned out to be one more fruitful stage in his artistic career.

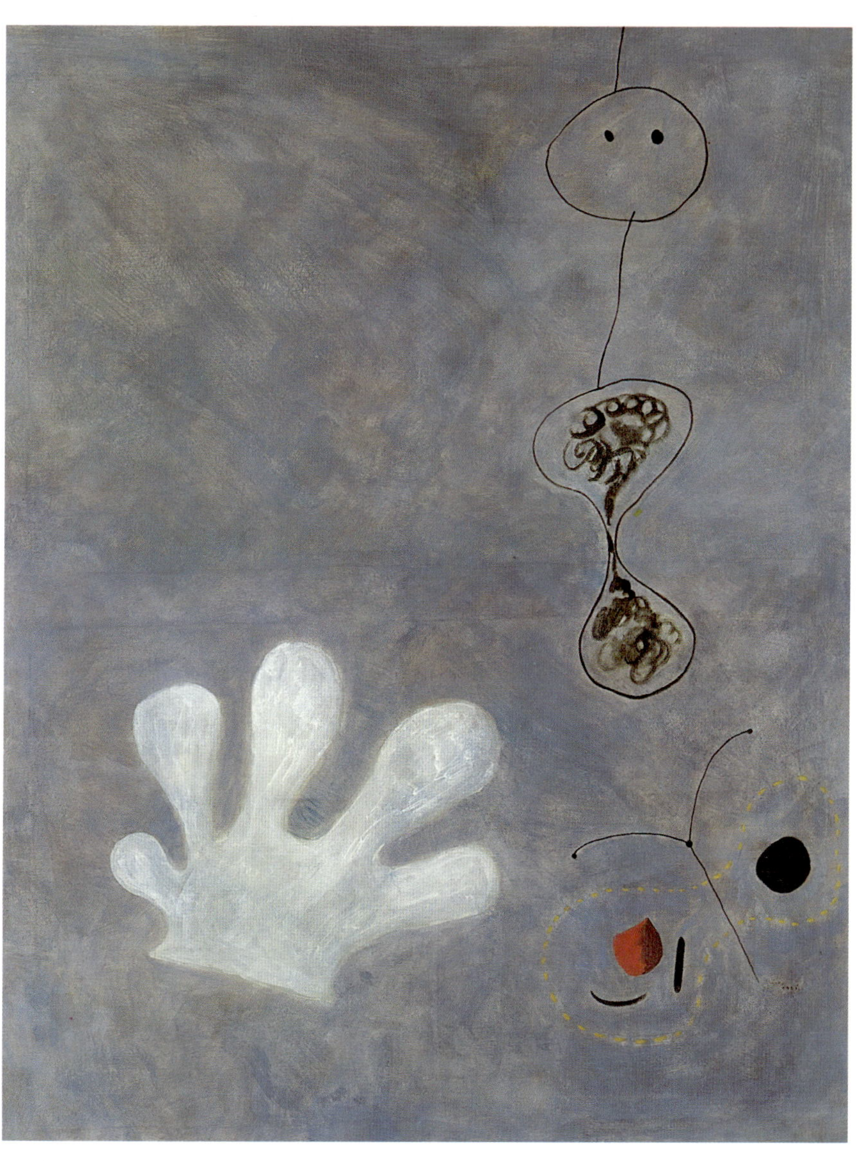

Painting (The white glove), 1925

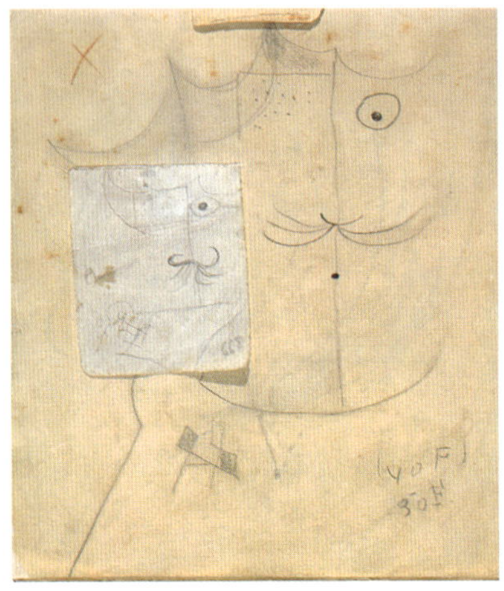

Preliminary sketch for *The music-hall usher*, 1925

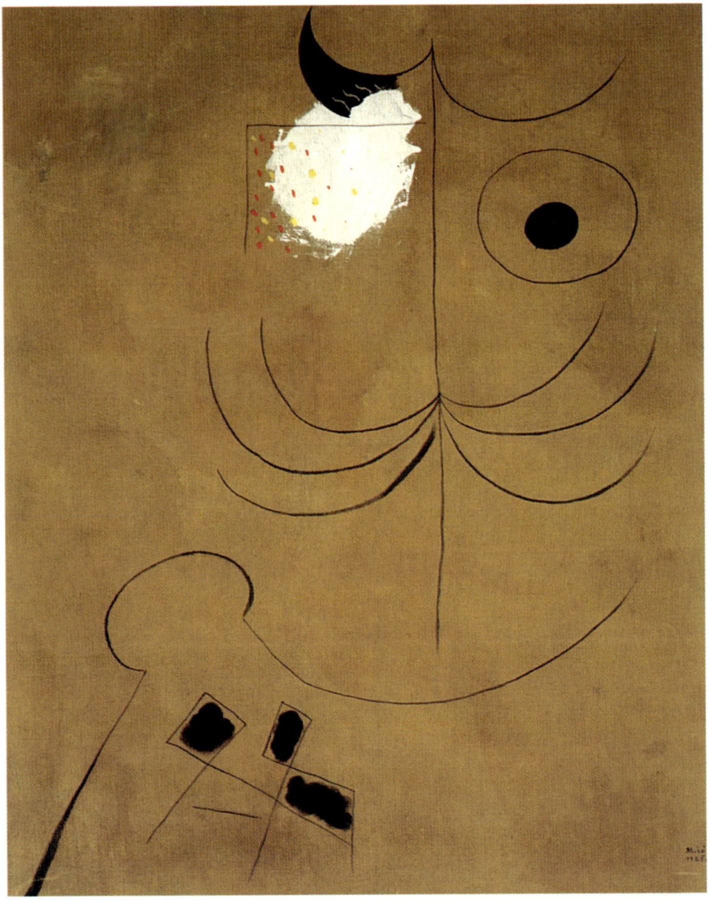

The music-hall usher, 1925. On permanent loan from the Generalitat de Catalunya

Dutch interior II, 1928. The Solomon R. Guggenheim Museum, New York

Postcard. The starting point for *Dutch interior II*, 1928

Preliminary sketch for *Dutch interior II*, 1928

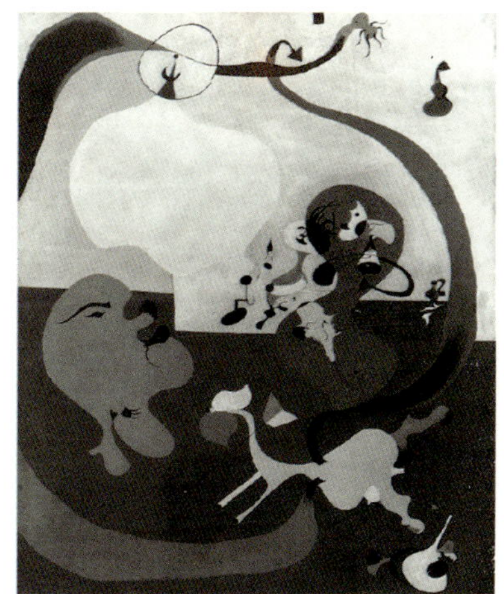

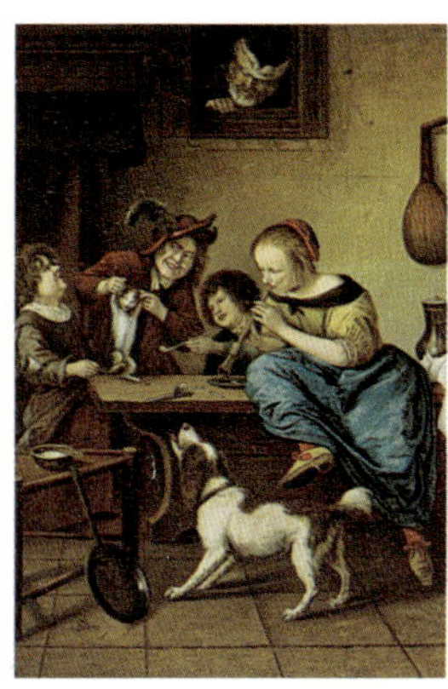

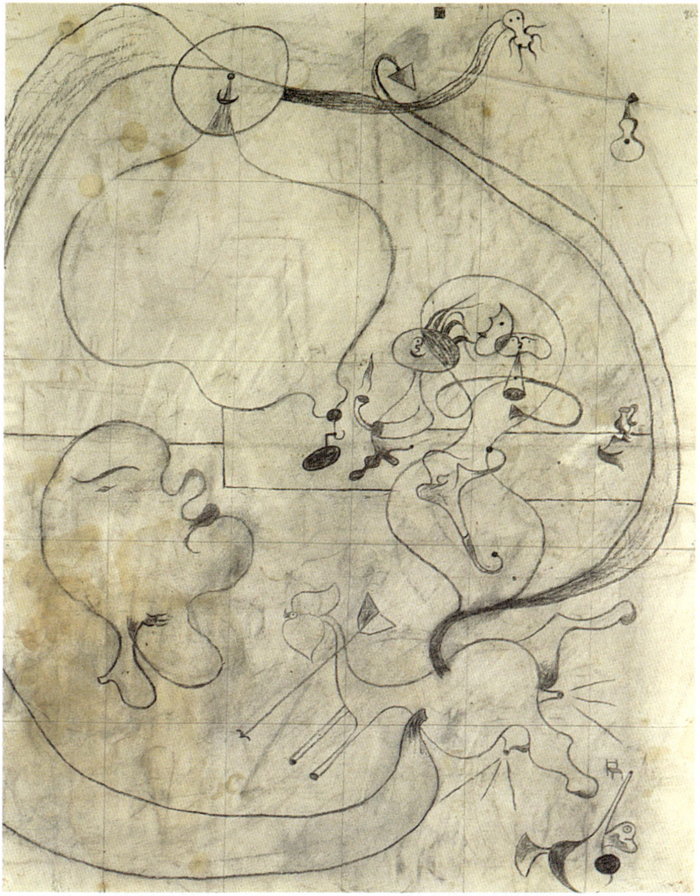

Portrait of Queen Louise of Prussia, 1929. Algur H. Meadows Collection, Southern Methodist University, Dallas, Texas

Preliminary sketch for *Portrait of Queen Louise of Prussia,* 1929

Preliminary sketch and advertisement, the starting point for *Portrait of Queen Louise of Prussia,* 1929

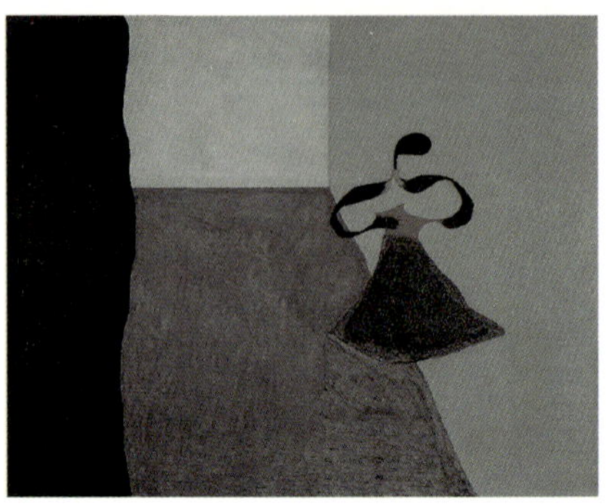

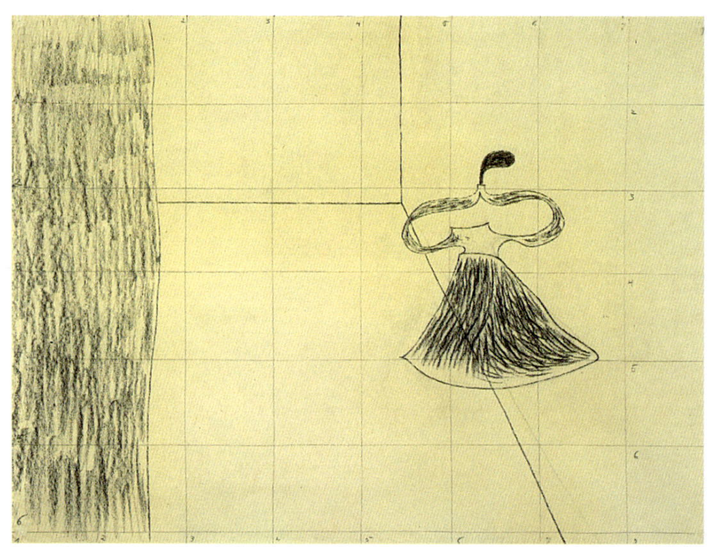

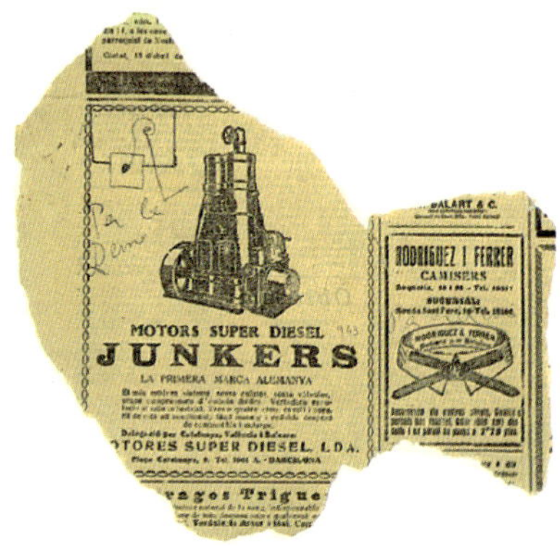

Preliminary sketch for
Untitled (Tree in the wind),
1929

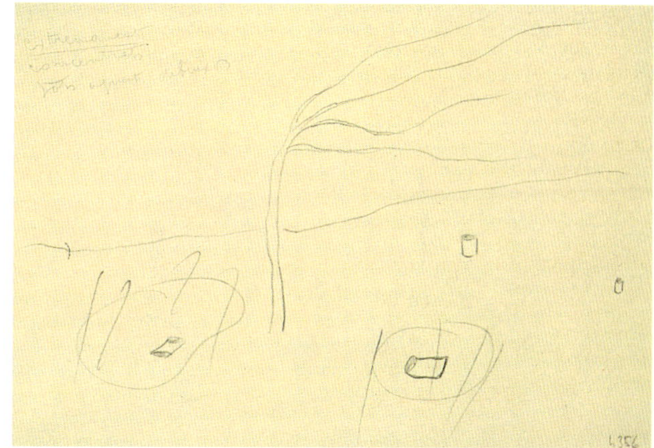

Untitled (Tree in the wind),
1929

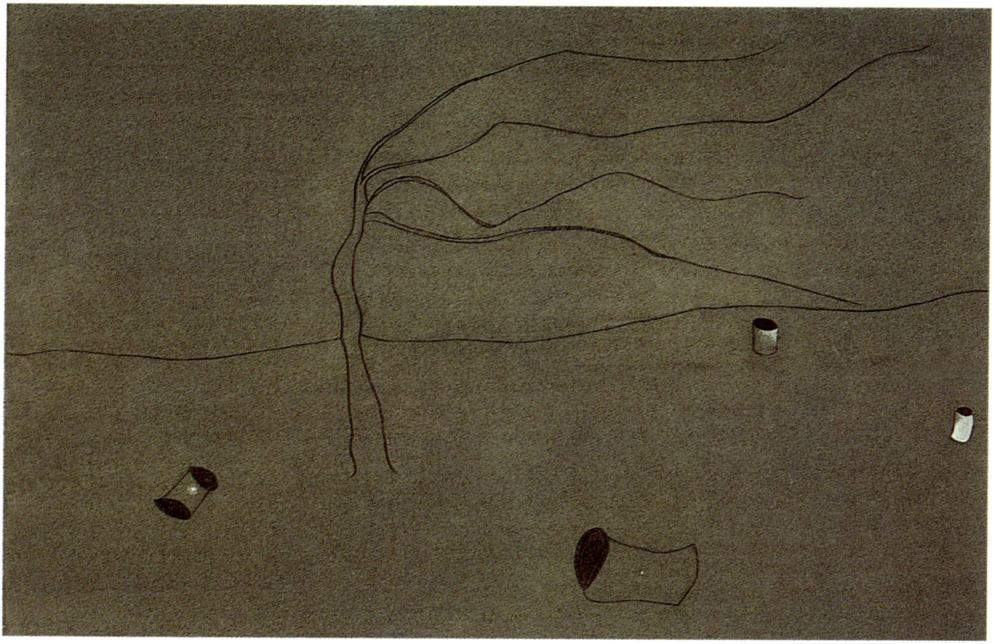

Composition with figures in a burning wood, 1931. Gift of David Fernández i Miró

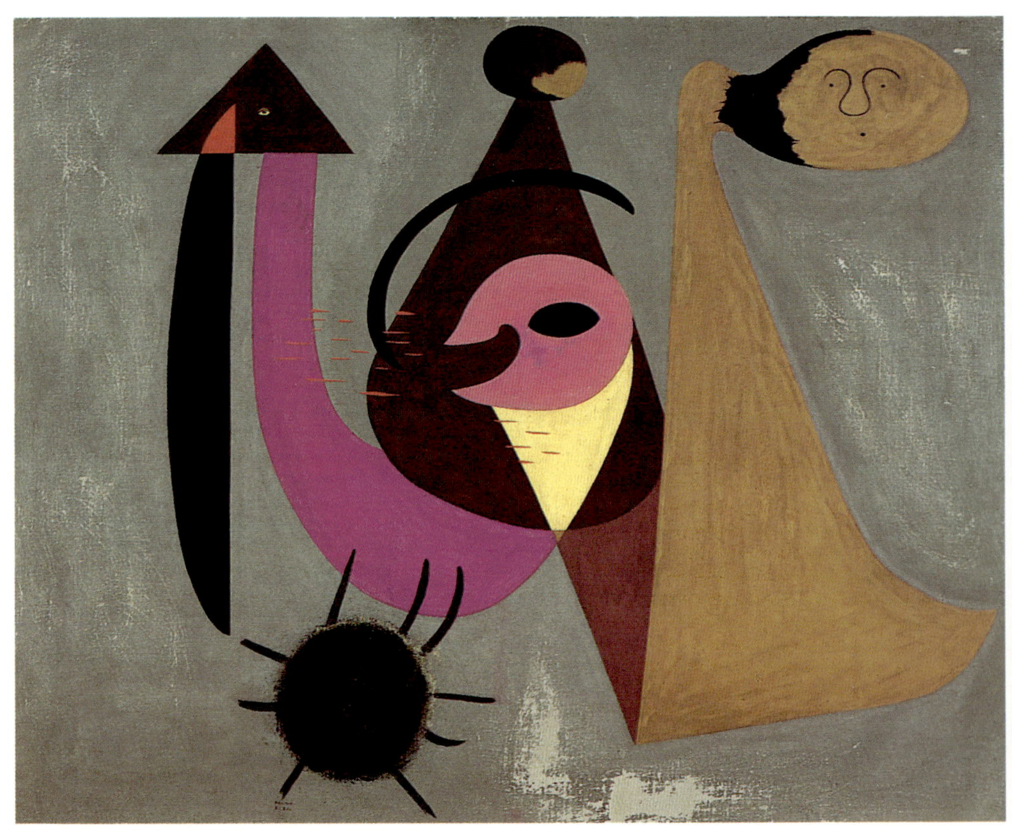

The Object in Space

For Miró, the beginning of the 1930s was a time of artistic crisis – already anticipated at the end of the 1920s – when he declared his desire to "assassinate painting". As a consequence, he sought alternative methods of expression that led to a new language and the investigation of other media such as collage, drawing, objects, etc.

The "Miró papers" also reflect this period during which the notes and jottings increased considerably as a result of the artist's reflections on his own work. On the other hand, the number of preliminary sketches for paintings fell in proportion, giving way to the drawings he produced in order to "build muscle", as he put it. Nonetheless, the ratio of preparatory sketches to finished works was still much the same.

The three-dimensional pieces that Miró produced in 1930 on the basis of objects, known as the *Constructions,* were to lead to one of his most gratifying experiences: working in the world of theatre.

In 1931, Boris Kochno, one of the artistic directors of the Ballets Russes de Montecarlo, saw Miró's *Constructions* exhibited at the Galerie Pierre in Paris. Deciding that these objects would be just right for the type of stage sets he envisaged for *Jeux d'enfants,* he immediately contacted Miró and commissioned him to design the sets and costumes for the ballet.

Miró already had some experience of working in the theatre, for in 1926, in collaboration with Max Ernst, he had painted the

Woman, 1930

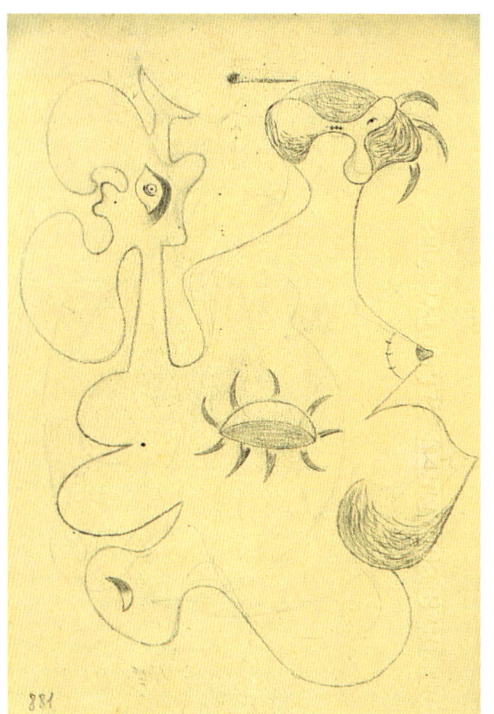

Study of costumes for the ballet *Jeux d'enfants*, 1932

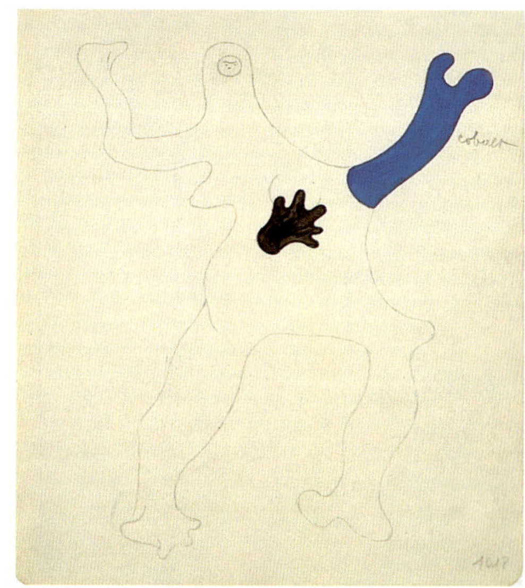

Painting on Ingres paper, 1932.
Gift of Joan Prats

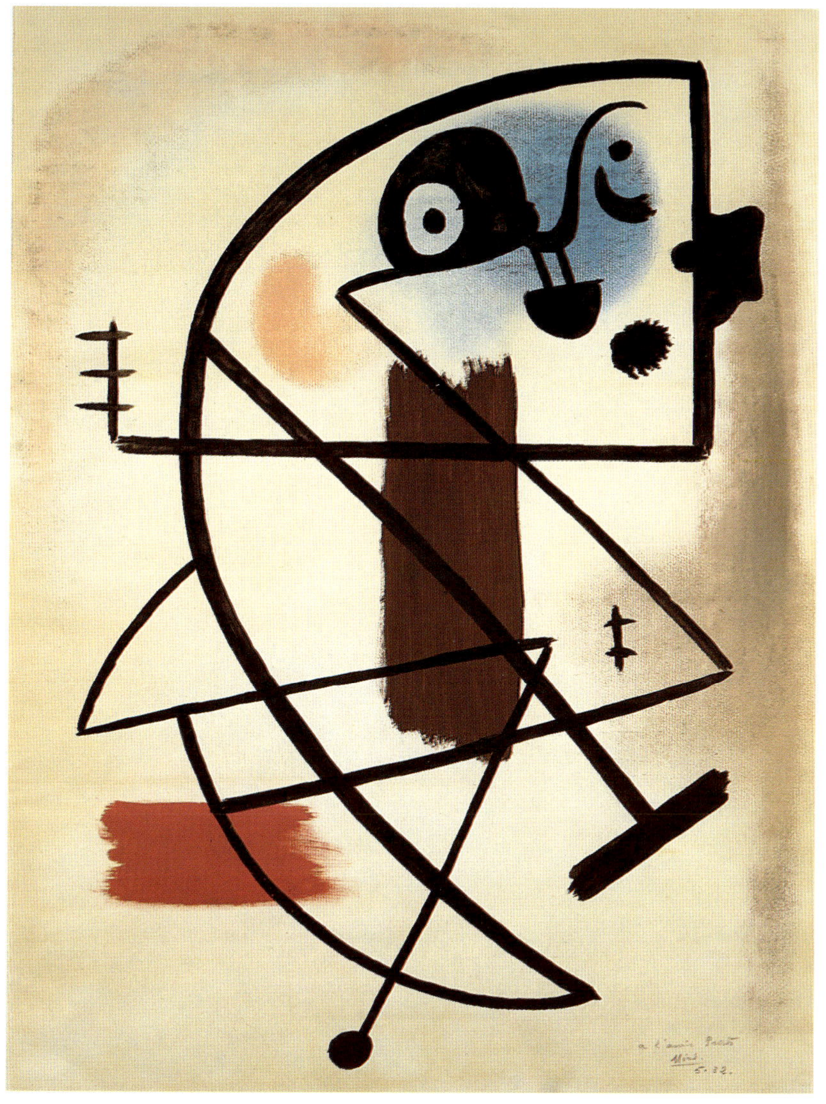

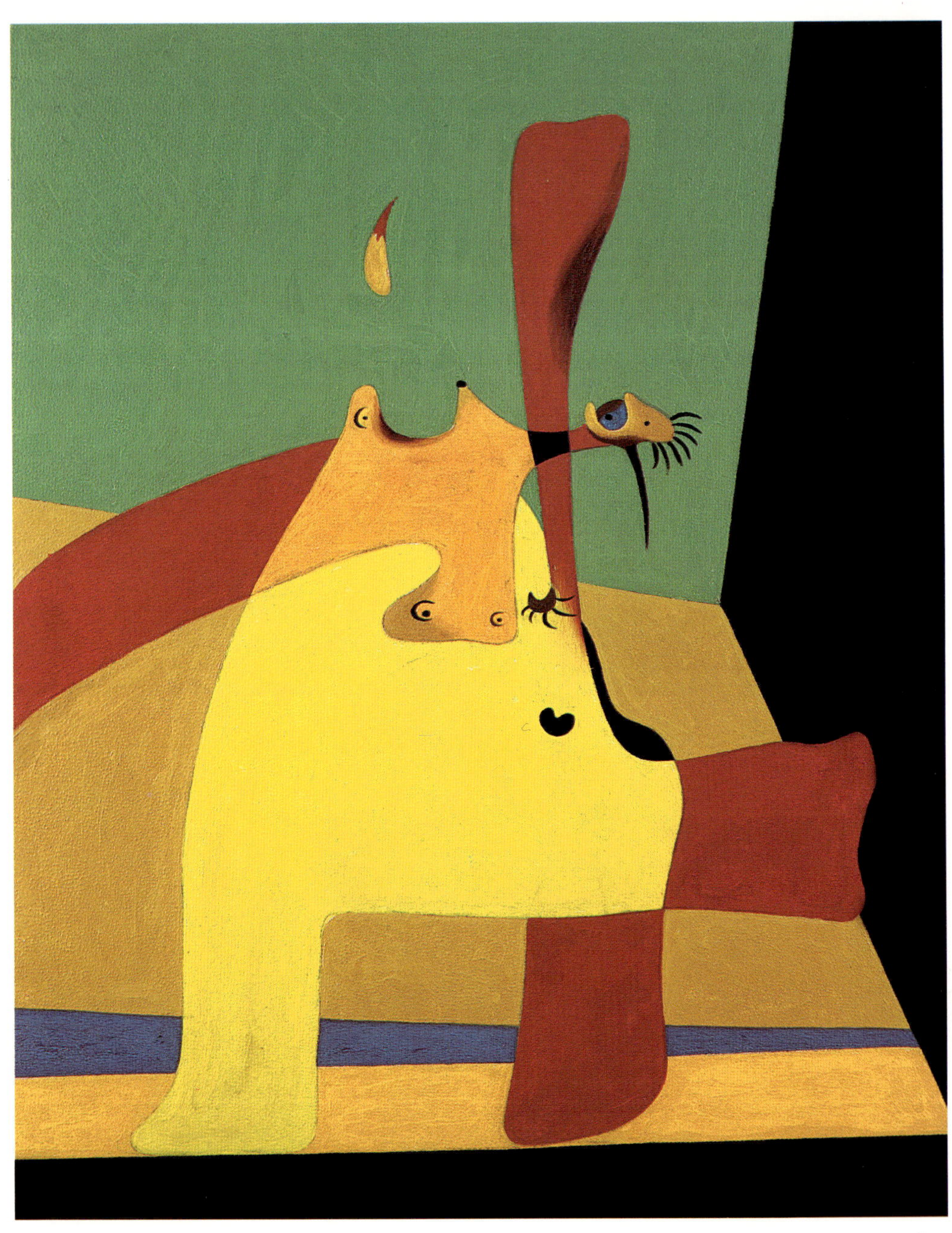

Flame in space and naked woman, 1932. Gift of Joan Prats

sets and designed the costumes and props for *Romeo and Juliet,* performed by the Ballets Russes. This time, however, the commission was a much more important one and he had to take sole responsibility for the work.

During the first three months of 1932, Miró worked hard on the ballet designs, and all this initial material – the preliminary sketches, notes and stage models – is currently held at the Foundation.

With music by Bizet, scenario by Boris Kochno, choreography by Léonide Massine and sets and costumes by Joan Miró, *Jeux d'enfants* had its highly successful premiere on 14th April 1932 at the Théâtre de Montecarlo.

The design of the proscenium curtain for this ballet is very similar to the series of paintings on Ingres paper started in 1931, one of which, from the Prats collection, is now at the Foundation.

During the time he spent in Mont-roig in 1932, Miró painted a number of small-format pictures, among them *Flame in space and naked woman.* These works are variations on the female form as seen from the artist's very individual perspective – a subject that predominated throughout his art and to which he devoted special attention during the 1930s.

Miró then changed to a larger format with the series of *Paintings based on a collage.* The preliminary stage of execution of each of these eighteen paintings, one of which is held at the Foundation, consisted in arranging the respective collages. Miró cut out newspaper advertisements and catalogue illustrations, then stuck them onto a sheet of laid paper. Using these compositions, devoid of any colour, he created a space in which to situate the forms deriving from the cut-out items, carefully establishing the relationship between each of them and the rest.

The choice of colours, the perfect balance between the forms, and the atmosphere produced by the ground, make the *Paintings based on a collage* one of the series in Miró's entire oeuvre that best demonstrates his reflective way of working.

In 1934, resorting once again to the collage technique, Miró produced a tribute to his friend Joan Prats. In an obvious reference to the latter's profession as a hatter, it consists of hats cut from an advertisement and a card reading "Prats is quality".

Preliminary collage for Painting, 1933

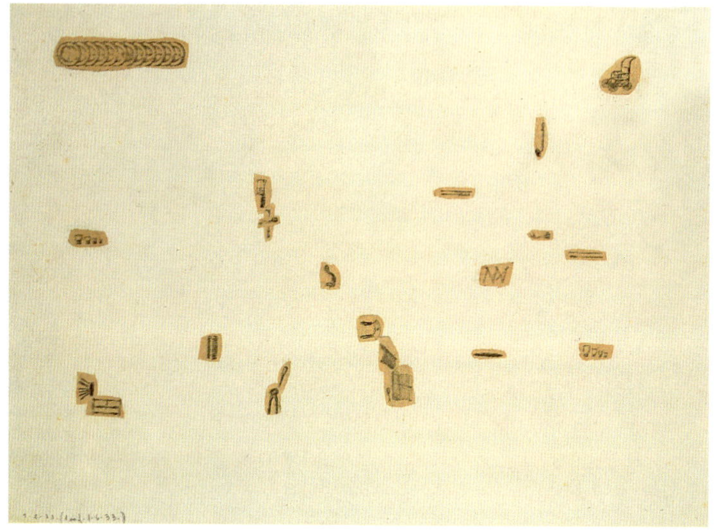

Here, the collage is not a separate item that determines the final composition but forms part of the finished picture along with the drawing.

Painting, 1933. On permanent loan from Maria Dolors Miró

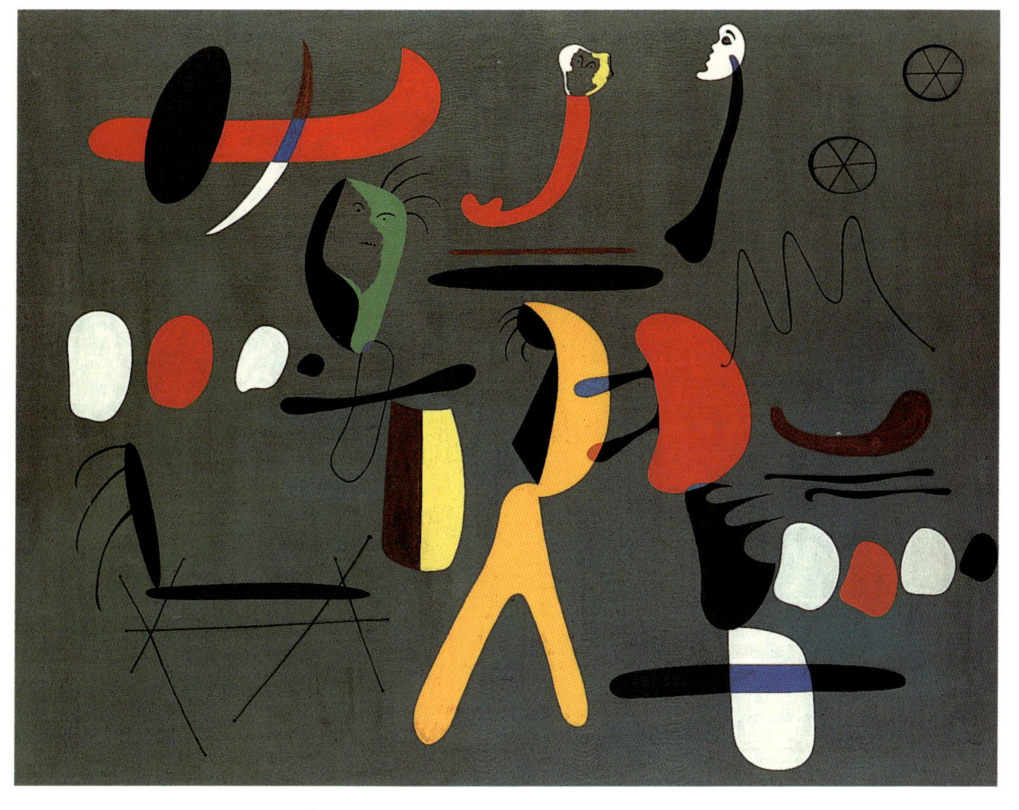

Collage-drawing (Homage to Prats), 1934. Gift of Joan Prats

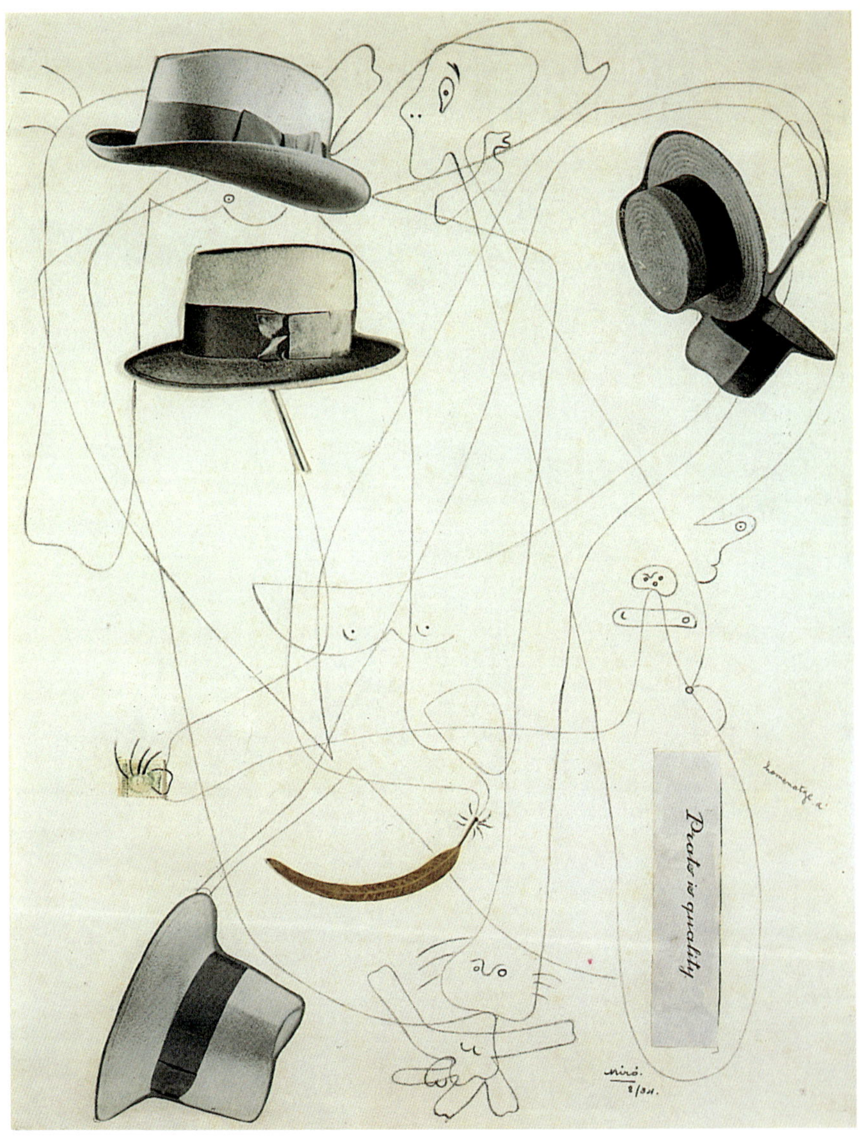

Painting, 1934. Gift of Joan Prats

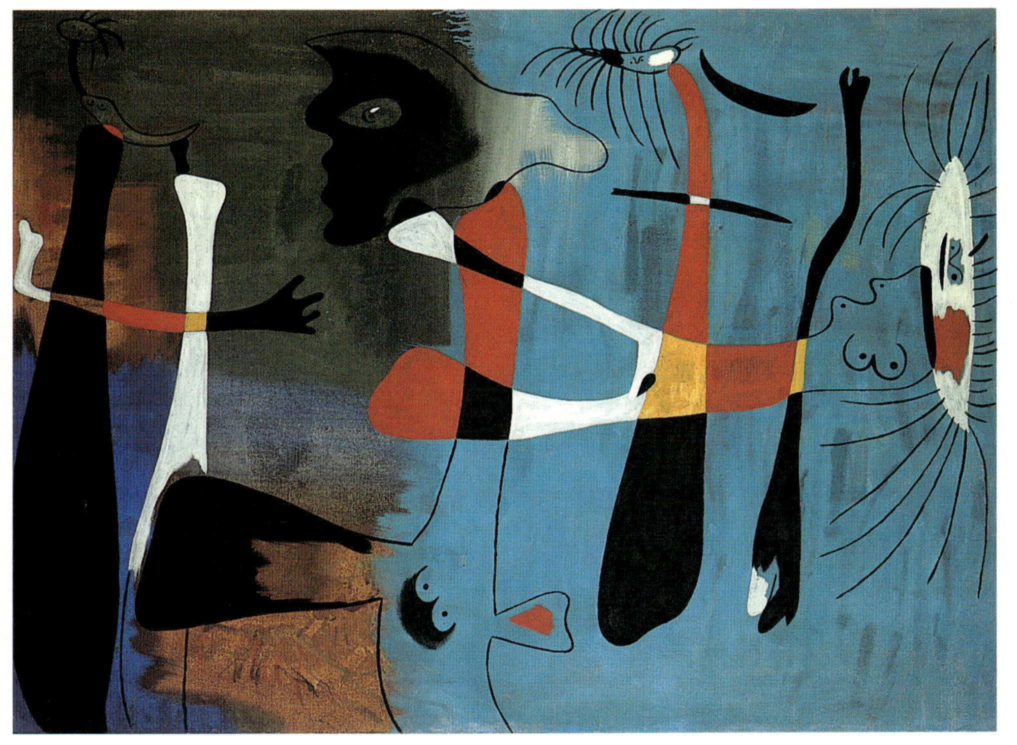

Design for a ballet curtain, 1935

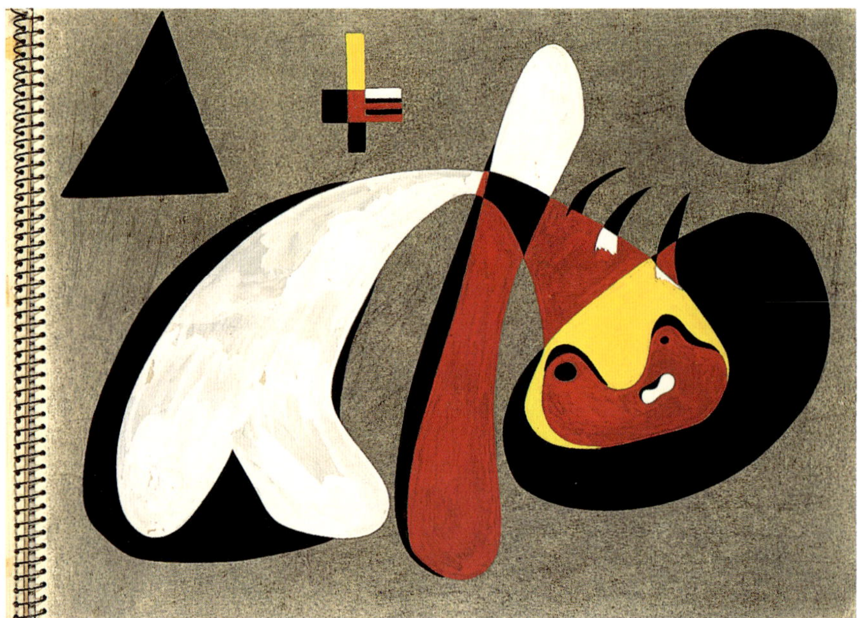

Man and woman in front of a pile of excrement, 1935. Gift of Pilar Juncosa de Miró

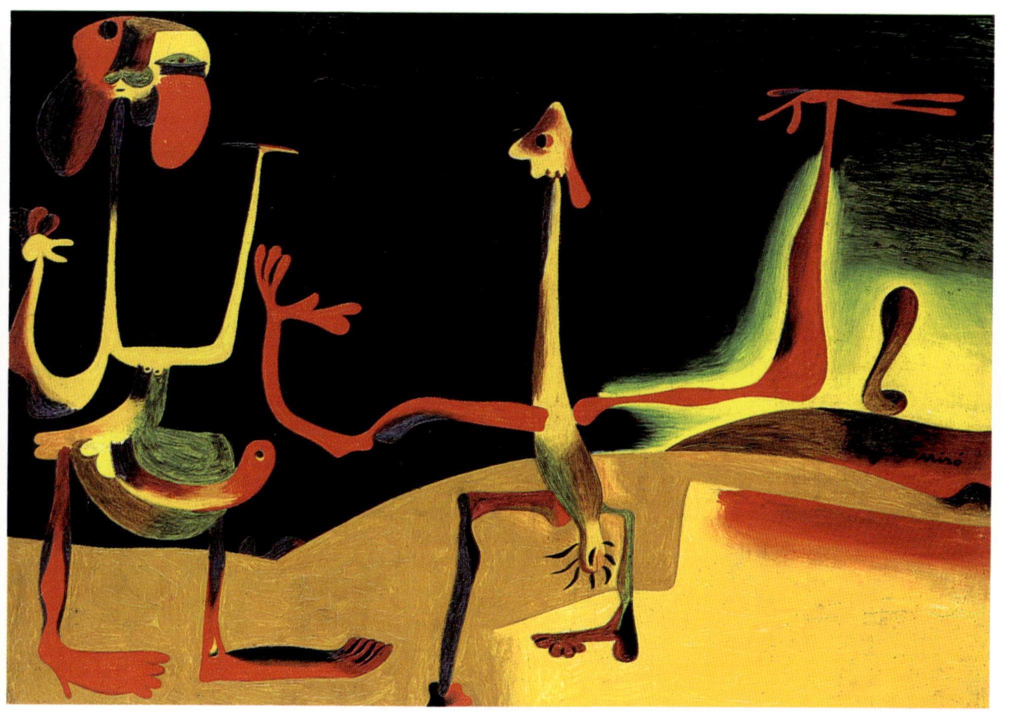

Painting on masonite, 1936. Gift of David Fernández i Miró

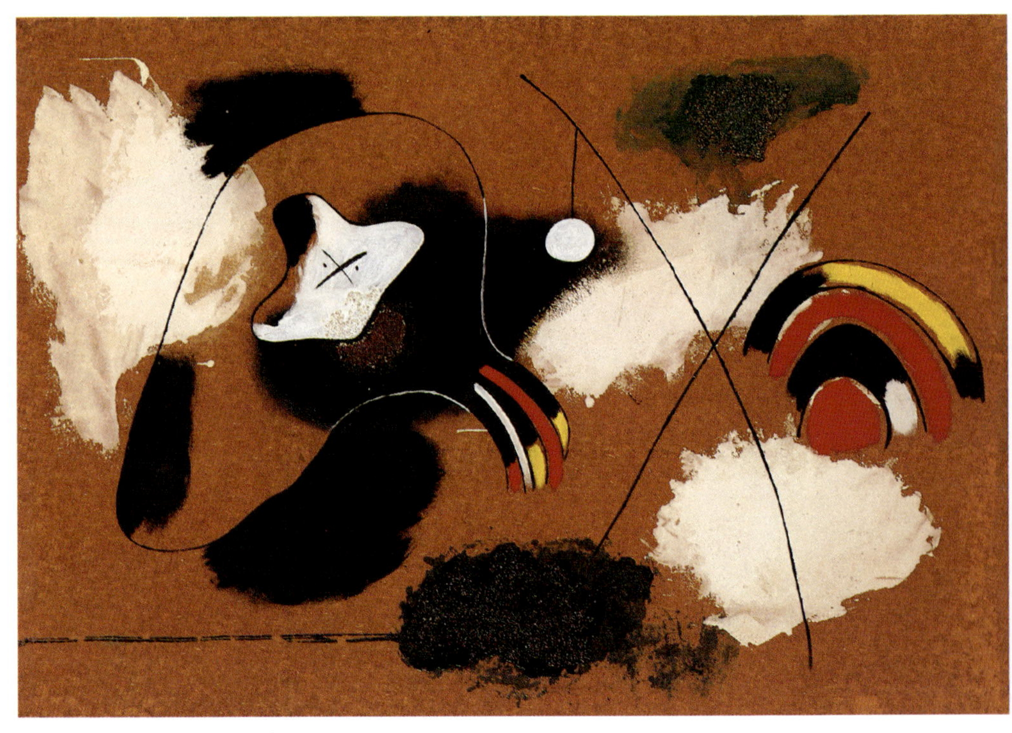

Synthesis

Following the outbreak of the Spanish Civil War, Miró expressed his opposition to it in a series of 27 paintings on masonite (a type of fibreboard). The aggressiveness is evident not only in the iconography but also in the act of painting itself: the unconventional support chosen – masonite – which is never completely covered, and the materials used in addition to oils, such as tar, sand, cascin and bitumen. The forms – which are unusual though identifiable within Miró's language – can be directly linked to those for *Jeux d'enfants*. The Foundation has one *Painting on masonite* as well as some of the preliminary sketches for the series.

In 1937, Miró, once again living in Paris, began attending life-drawing classes at the Académie de la Grande Chaumière.

At a time when he was suffering on account of the dramatic events in Spain, he again approached the problem of the human figure, and his feelings can be guessed in the tortured forms he drew at the Paris art school. It was in this same spirit that he produced the grotesque *Naked woman climbing a staircase.*

Coinciding with this return to figurative representation, Miró designed the stencil *Aidez l'Espagne* – the preparatory sketch for which is held by the Foundation – in order to collect funds to help the Republican side in the Civil War. At the same time he also painted *The reaper* for the Spanish Republic Government's pavilion at the Paris World Fair in 1937.

Male nude and female nude,
1937

Naked woman climbing a staircase,
1937

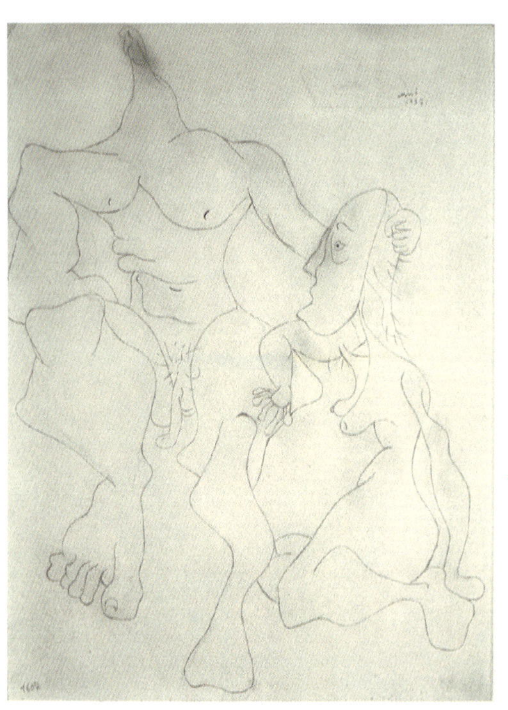

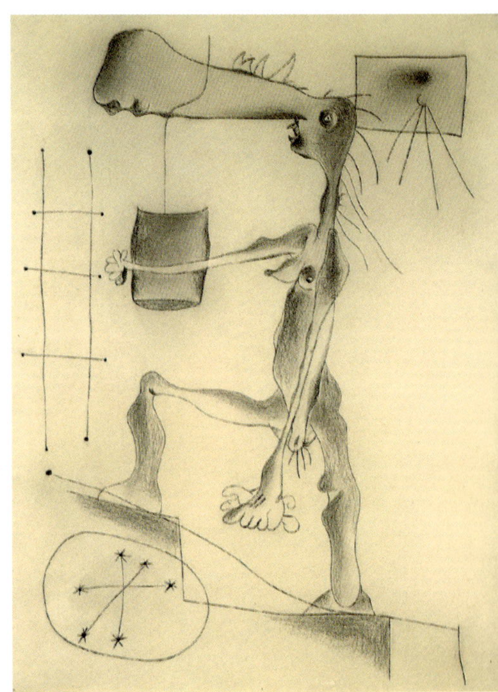

Aidez l'Espagne, 1937

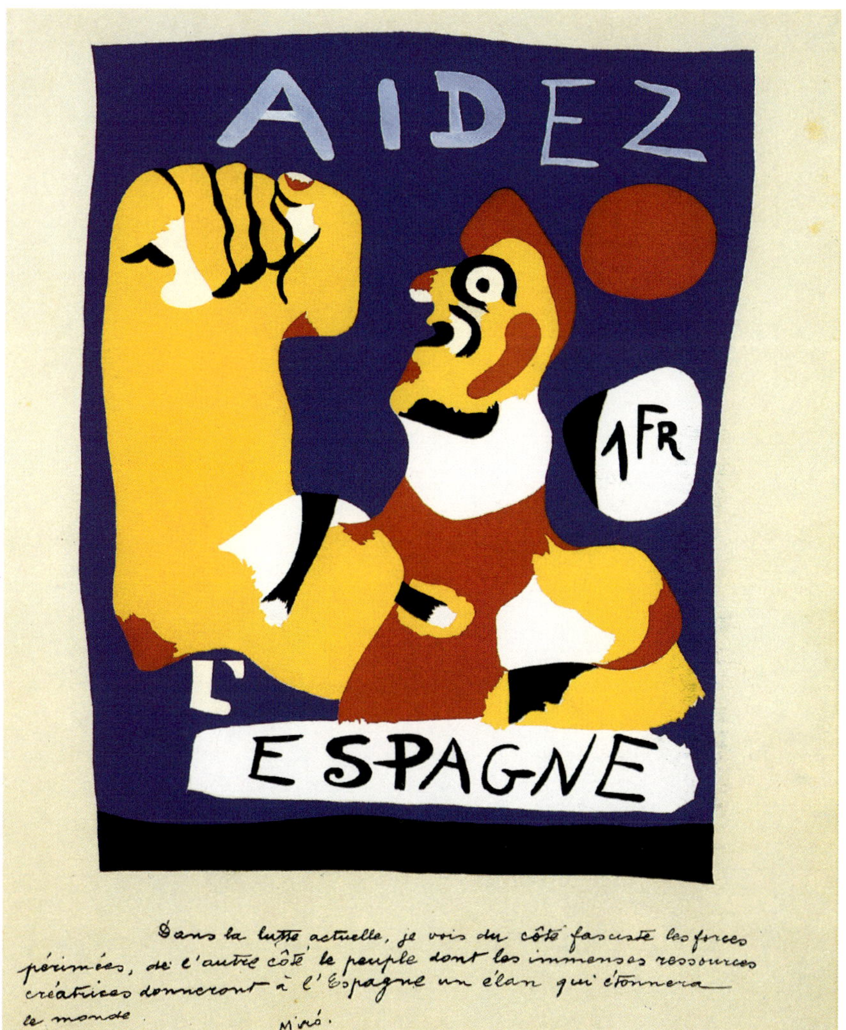

Luis Lacasa and Josep Lluís Sert were the architects commissioned to design the pavilion, and the artists involved in it worked in close conjunction with them. Picasso painted *Guernica,* Calder designed the *Mercury fountain* – now at the Foundation – Julio González produced the sculpture *Montserrat* and Alberto presented *The Spanish people have a path that leads to a star.*

Miró painted *The reaper* on six panels of celotex – the material covering the inside of the pavilion – measuring a total of 5.50 x 3.65 metres. This was his first monumental work, but unfortunately it disappeared when it was dismantled along with the pavilion and no trace of it remains other than a few photographs.

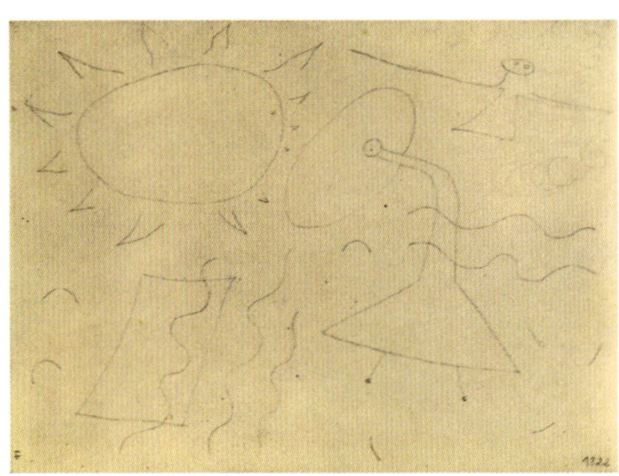

Preliminary sketch for *The flight of a bird over the plain IV,* 1939

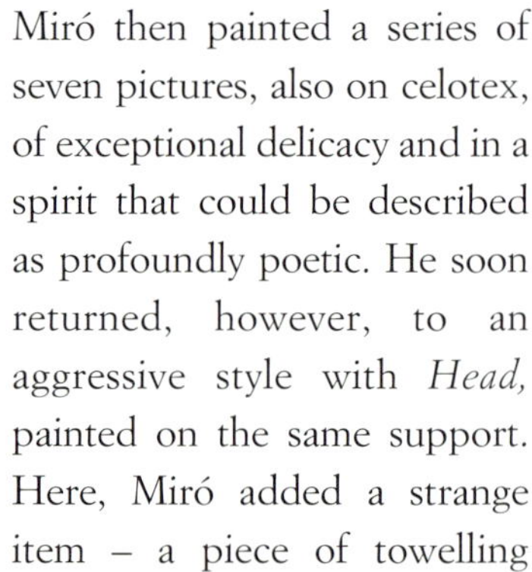

In contrast to this piece, Miró then painted a series of seven pictures, also on celotex, of exceptional delicacy and in a spirit that could be described as profoundly poetic. He soon returned, however, to an aggressive style with *Head,* painted on the same support. Here, Miró added a strange item – a piece of towelling stiffened with glue, stuck to the surface of the fibreboard. The vibrant texture of the piece emphasises its brutal appearance.

Little by little Miró again abandoned figurative representation for signs and symbols and concentrated his attention on the sky rather than on his immediate surroundings. Thus, from notes made in the margins of a sheet of newspaper during a train journey in 1939 from Paris to Varengeville-sur-Mer on the Normandy coast, he painted the series of *Flight of a bird over the plain.*

As a result of the start of the Second World War, Miró decided to remain in Normandy with his family, and it was there that he began the *Constellations* series. The first piece, titled *Sunrise*, is dated in Varengeville on 20th January 1940. The twenty-third and final one, *The passage of the divine bird*, was painted in Mont-roig on 12th September 1941.

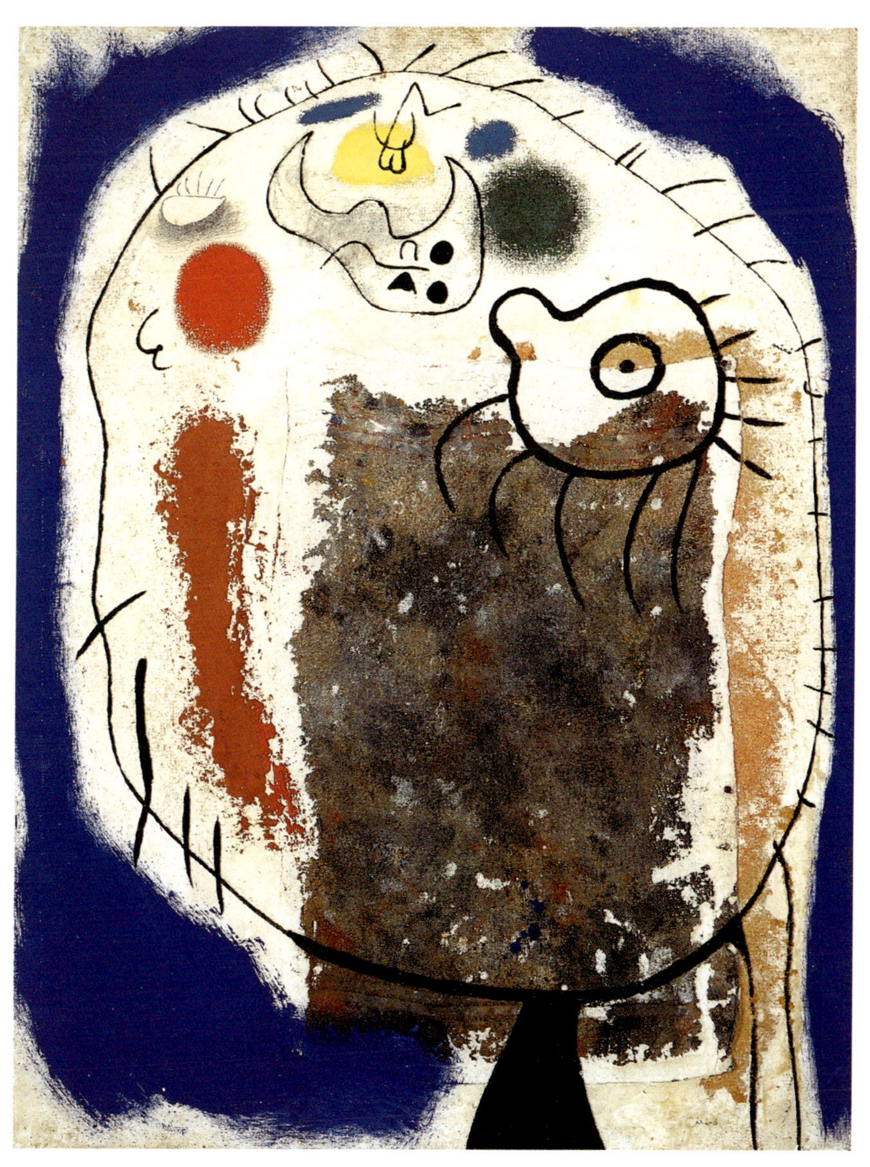

Head, 1937

The *Constellations,* all of which were painted on paper, occupy a key place in Miró's oeuvre, for they signify a new challenge in resolving the pictorial problems he faced, namely the definition of forms and the consolidation of a particular subject matter.

The initial operation consisted in wetting the paper and rubbing it in order to roughen the surface. He then applied the ground colour, which graduates gently from one tone to another, while maintaining a transparent effect that creates a delicate, subtle atmosphere.

The forms come from the preceding years but are less aggressive. The figures are no longer cruel and isolated but linked by a kind of network of lines that gives shape to the composition and removes any trace of violence.

In this complexity of forms, colour plays a fundamental role. The range used by Miró is extremely limited: often just three or four pure colours alongside the various tones of black. The colour is systematically subordinated to the form, while the superimposition of forms brings about a change of colour in overlapping areas. This particular distribution of colour is one of the typical features of Miró's work and resulted in his highly personal chequered effects.

The iconography of the *Constellations* seems to represent the entire cosmic order. The figures symbolise the earth, and the stars refer to the infinite world of the heavens, of which we have only a visual or tactile experience. The birds and the ladder of escape act as the link between the terrestrial world and the celestial world, the source of imagination.

The Foundation holds one of the *Constellations* series, *Morning star,* which Joan Miró gave as a present to his wife, Pilar Juncosa, and which after his death she generously donated to the Foundation.

Miró made no preparatory sketches for the *Constellations,* but let each composition suggest itself from a minute flaw in the paper or from the presence of one element that naturally seemed to call for another.

This method of working directly on to the paper in a unpremeditated way was employed by Miró in parallel with

Morning star, 1940. Gift of Pilar Juncosa de Miró

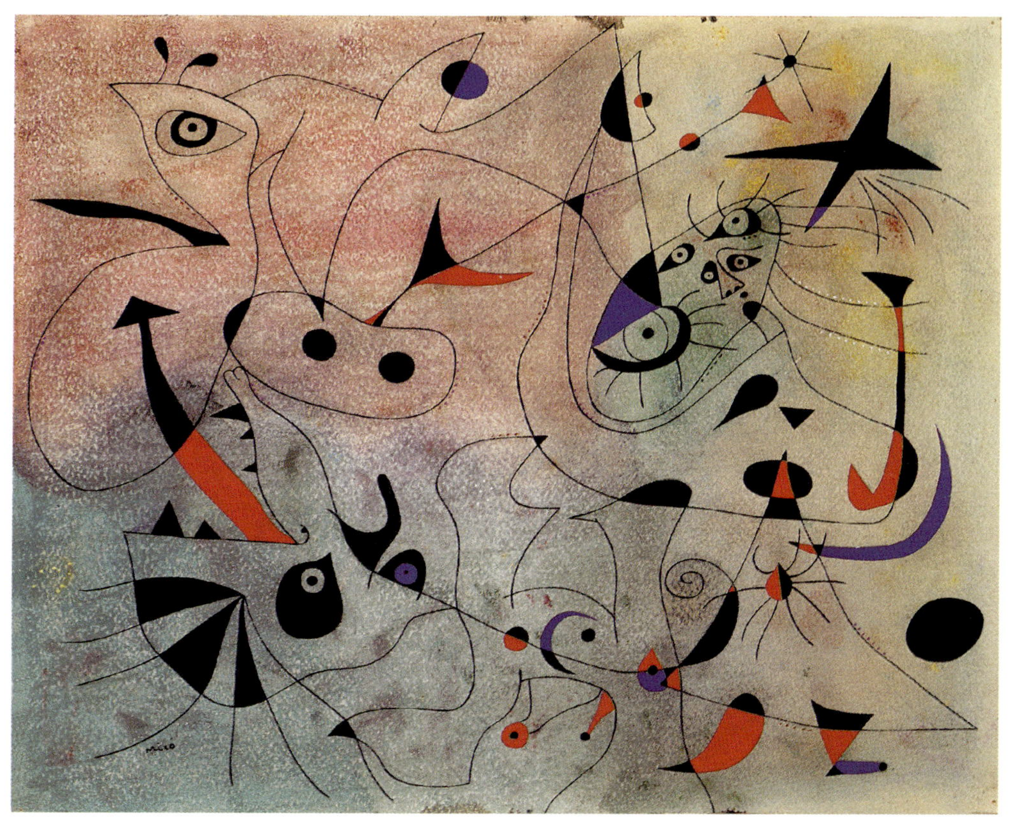

another more systematic and disciplined method reflected in the sketchbooks of the time, produced in Varengeville and Palma, with the date and time meticulously recorded.

Woman, whom the artist treats in a generic rather than an individualised manner, is the subject of most of the drawings in these sketchbooks. She is also the central theme of another exceptional set of works from the same period – the *Barcelona series.*

While Miró was working "overtly" on the *Constellations*, with their lyrical, open spirit and bright colours – he often mentioned them in his correspondence at that time with Pierre Matisse – he was "covertly" producing the *Barcelona series,* of an epic nature, with strong dramatic content and extremely austere colouring.

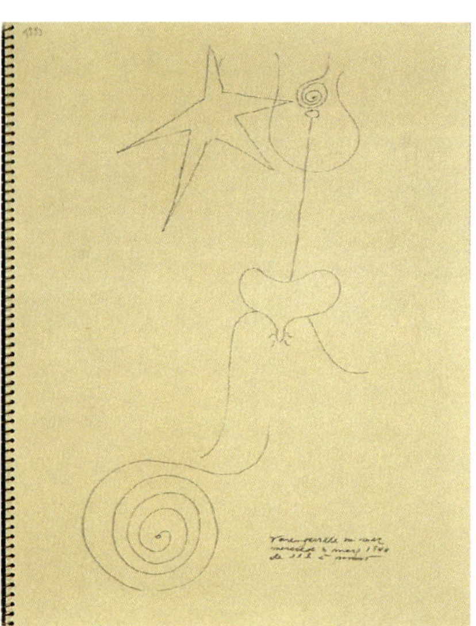

Dancer,
1940

He could never have imagined that the drawings on transfer paper, with a wide range of tones from black to grey, would one day be transferred to lithographic stone. It was thanks to the help of Joan Prats that despite the precarious post-war situation the complete series was able to be published. The edition was limited to five copies of each print, and the Foundation holds one complete set together with the various proofs and states, donated respectively by Joan Prats and Joan Miró.

The *Constellations* and the *Barcelona series,* produced simultaneously but so different in appearance, have in common the fact that they are both based on the same subjects – woman, birds and heavenly bodies – which were to be the themes of Miró's later output, from painting to ceramics.

Lithograph from the *Barcelona series,* 1944

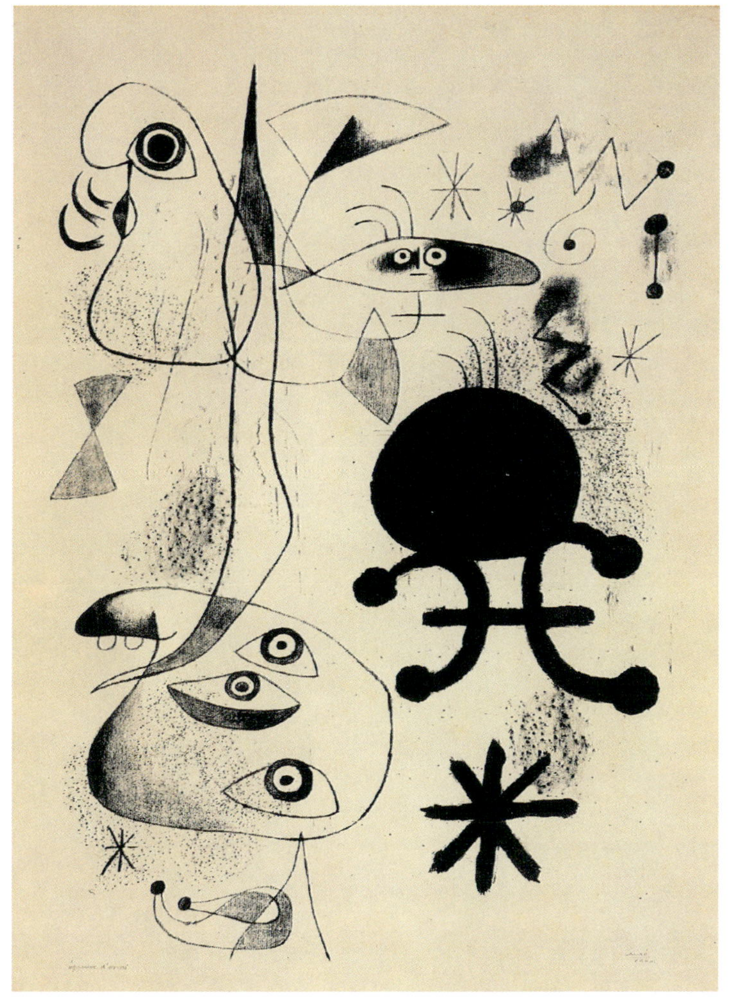

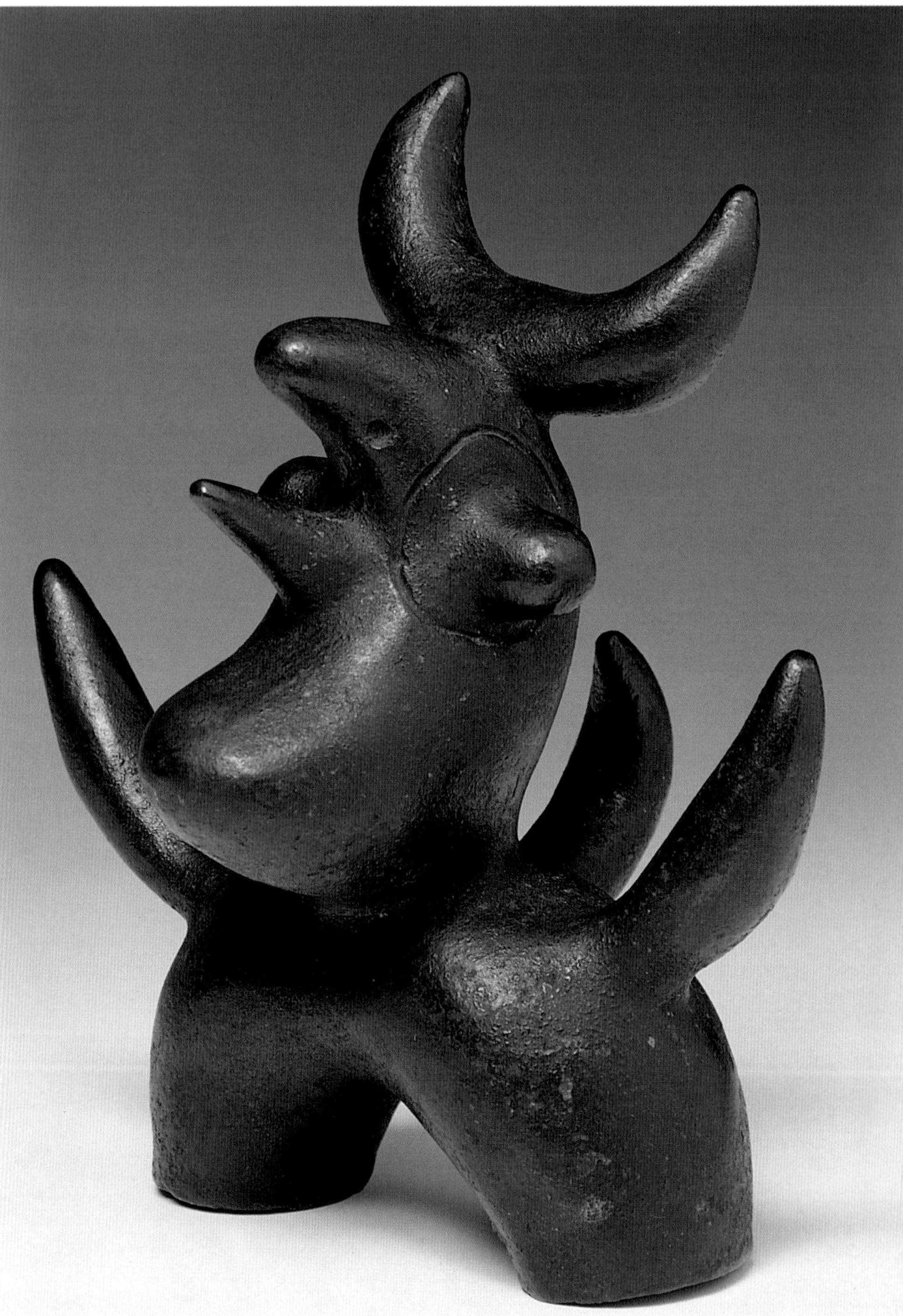

Plenitude

After completing the *Constellations* series in 1941, Miró continued using paper as the main support for the works he was to produce over the next two years. By this time he had a thorough knowledge of the secrets of painting techniques and a mastery of his own particular pictorial language.

Having reached this point in his development, he was anxious to explore the possibilities offered by other techniques and media. Thus for a period of ten years starting in 1944, when he began working on ceramics, he divided his time between painting and other forms of expression. In 1946 he produced his first sculptures in bronze.

1947 saw the appearance of Miró's first colour lithographs, at the Mourlot studio in Paris. Shortly afterwards he began the woodcuts for one of his most important illustrated books, *À toute épreuve,* containing poems by Paul Éluard and published by Gérald Cramer.

Miró's output as a result of the new paths he explored during this time continued to have close links, as regards form and content, with painting, which was always at the origin of his discoveries.

The subject matter of the works from this period was taken directly from the *Constellations.* The constant themes continued to be woman, birds and stars, which we find in *Woman and bird in the night, Woman dreaming of escape,*

Moon bird,
1946

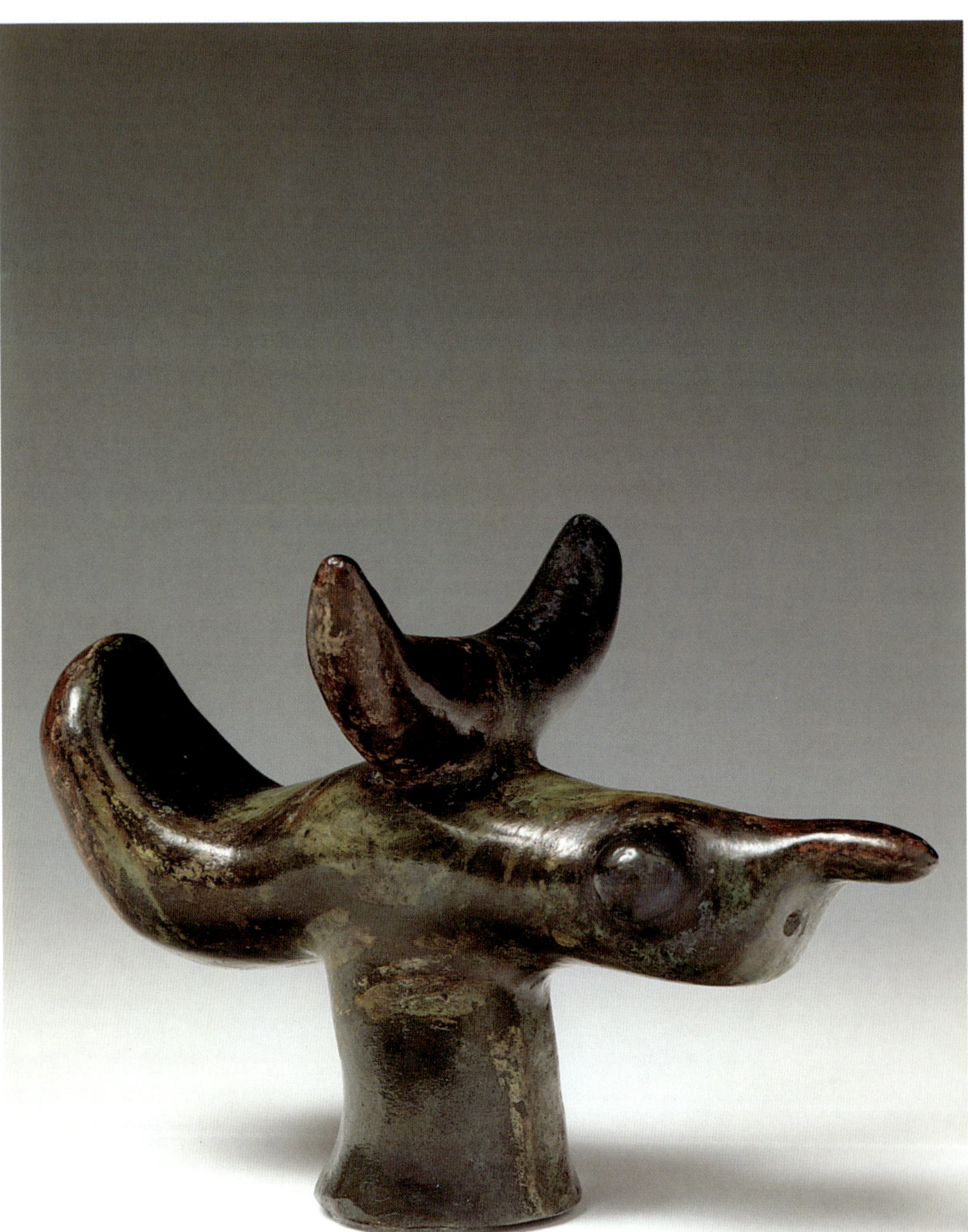

Sun bird, 1946

Woman and birds at daybreak and *Morning star.* His formal vocabulary also had its roots in the *Constellations,* but these later works were more simplified than the previous ones: forms became larger and more individualised, and the typical network of lines in the *Constellations* disappeared.

One innovation at this time was the appearance of figures on different scales, such as can be seen in *Painting in art nouveau frame.* Similarly, we find the first juxtaposition of carefully worked fine lines and almost gestural marks in thick brush strokes. Gesture becomes more apparent in paintings such as *The diamond smiles at twilight,* anticipating the predominance of the firm free-hand stroke in later works.

In 1956, Miró settled in Palma (Majorca), where he began working in the spacious studio designed for him by his friend the architect Josep Lluís Sert. He had finally realised his dream of having a large studio, which he had described in an article titled "Je rêve d'un grand atelier", published in *XXe Siècle* in 1938.

In order to create an agreeable atmosphere, he started collecting all manner of objects that might be of interest in his work, from newspaper cuttings to roots picked up during a walk along the beach, pieces of vernacular art, shells, old farm implements and so on. Gradually he got his new workplace together. However, his almost exclusive dedication to print-making, lithography and ceramics, which completely absorbed him for five years, left him no time to fully enjoy the new studio until 1958.

During this period Miró felt a need to branch out in new directions, so as not to remain stuck with a single image of his work, which had by then become well known. His first move was to go through all the preliminary sketches and drawings he had made throughout his life. He then produced new versions of many of them, which he kept beside the originals and which have survived as testimony to a way of working that led him to express himself plainly and directly. He would as easily be carried away by the force of a mark made in a single impulsive gesture as by the delicate lines contrasting with the matter and patches of colour.

Woman and bird in the night,
1945. On permanent loan from
Joan Punyet i Miró

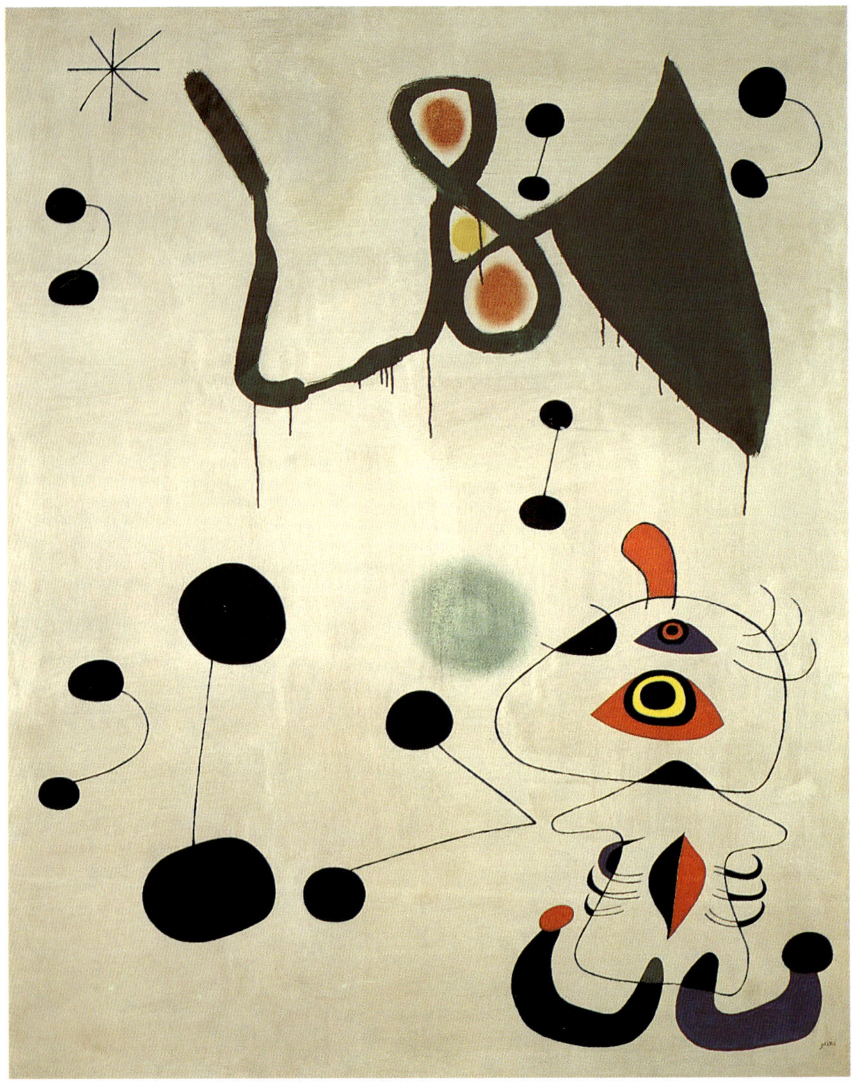

Woman dreaming of escape,
1945

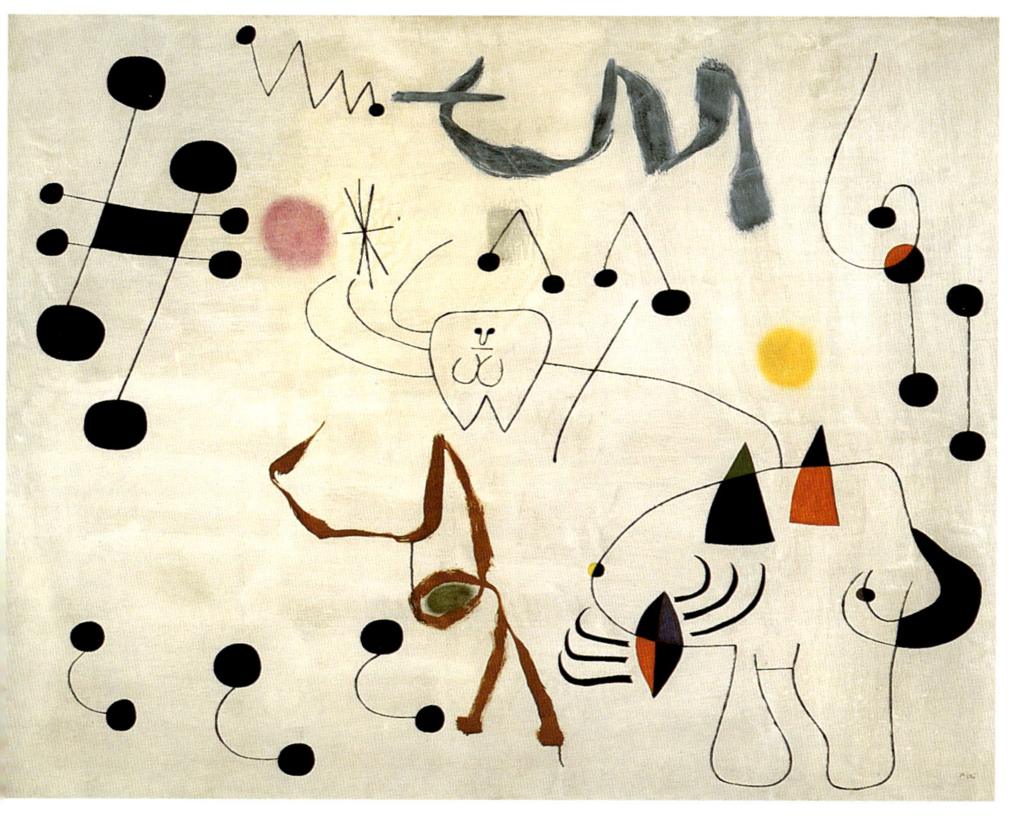

Morning star, 1946. On permanent loan from Teodor Punyet i Miró

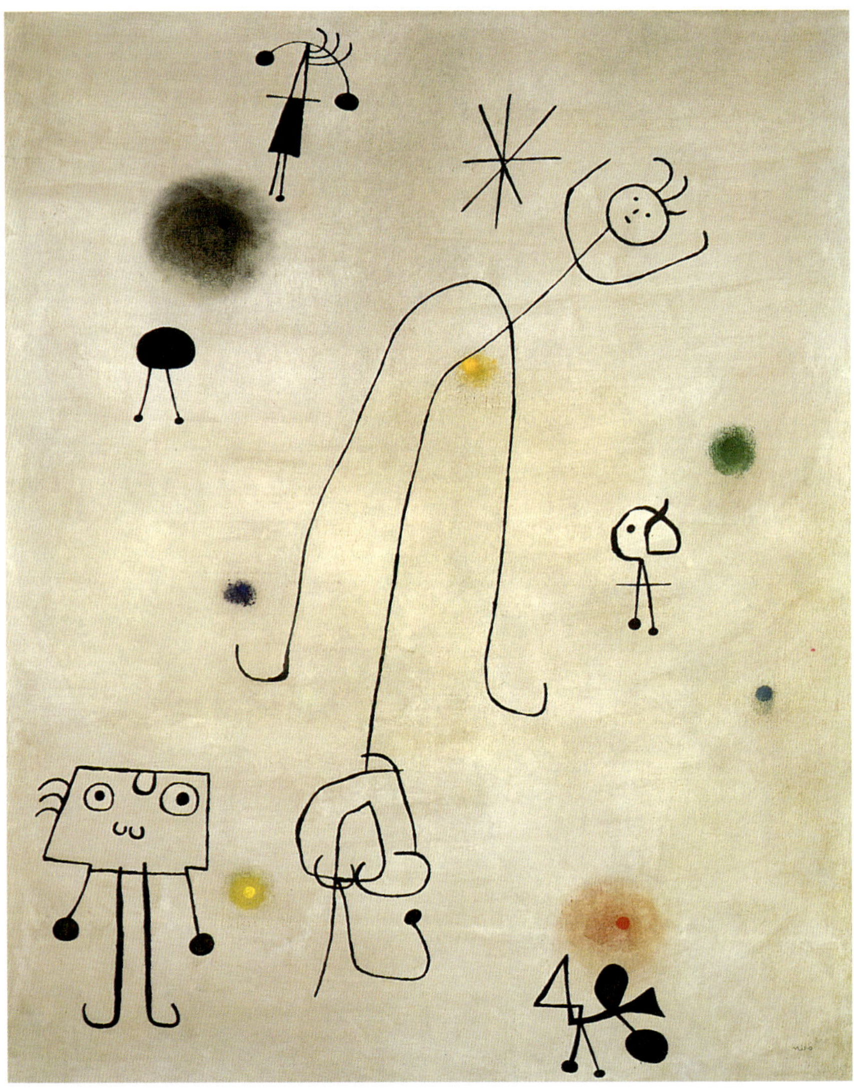

Woman and birds at daybreak,
1946. On permanent loan from
Emili Fernández i Miró

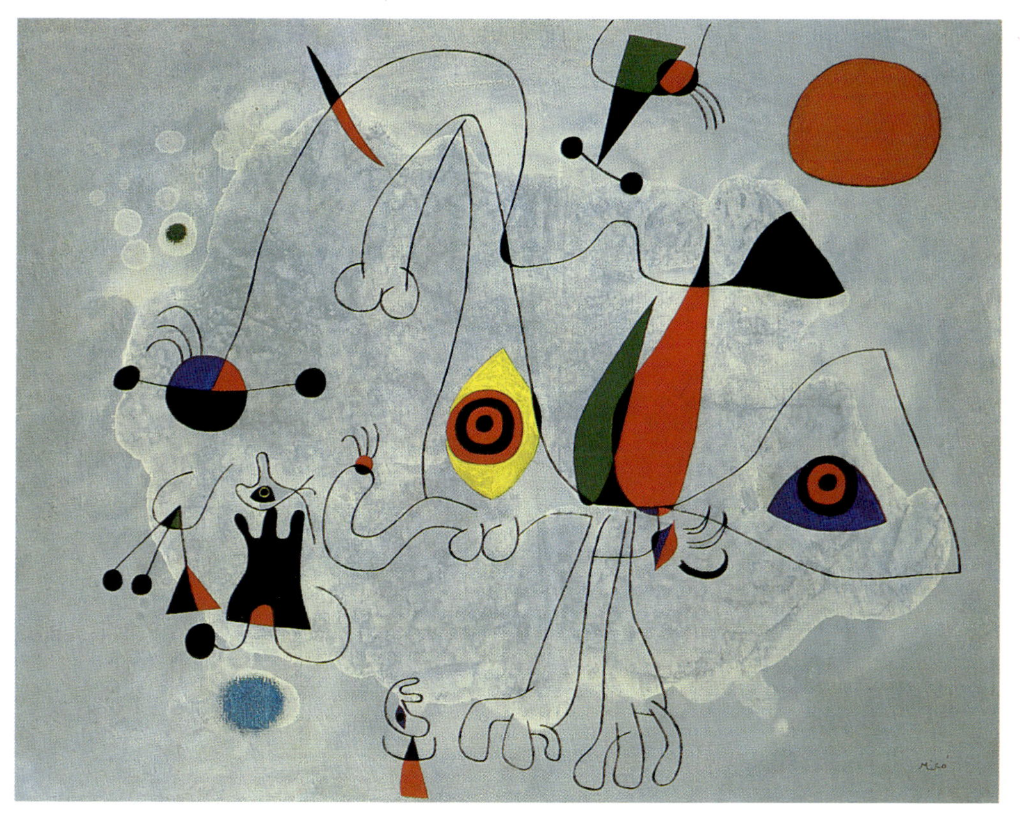

Without losing its overall consistency, Miró's art underwent a rupture manifested in the predominance of gesture and marks over signs.

His reworking of the 1937-38 *Self-portrait* is a clear example of the end of an era. In the original piece, he had portrayed himself in a pencil drawing on canvas with a profusion of lines reproducing every single detail of his face. In 1960, using an exact reproduction of *Self-portrait*, Miró produced the version that is now held at the Foundation. On top of the original drawing, he highlighted the essential features of the portrait in thick, firm, black strokes – the head, hair, eyes, neck and shoulders – with a minimal application of colour.

Sureness of gesture in his work, which as Miró grew older became more accentuated, was never incompatible with the subtlety that also characterised it, and this is particularly apparent in the works on paper. An example is *Woman in a pretty hat* also from 1960.

The fact that Miró's language became increasingly direct did not preclude the use of preliminary sketches as a way of visualising an idea before committing it to canvas. Even paintings such as *Blue I, II, III* or *Flight of the dragonfly in front of the sun,* where colour is the predominant element of the composition, were done from preparatory sketches. Another characteristic feature of the drawings of the last twenty-five years of the artist's life is the absence of the intimacy of the earlier period. On the other hand, like the paintings, they gained in immediacy.

A further aspect to be noted in connection with colour is the consolidation of black and white, not merely as complementary colours but as colours in their own right on Miró's palette. Following the tradition of drawing, he often used white as the ground and usually black as the vehicle for writing. By the late 1960s, the presence of black had become very much more evident, and it is often the colour used to organise the composition and determine the distribution of the other colours. Examples of this are *Figure in front of the sun,* where the black defines the presence of the two items in the title of the picture, and *Catalan peasant in the moonlight.*

Painting in art nouveau frame,
1943. Gift of Joan Prats

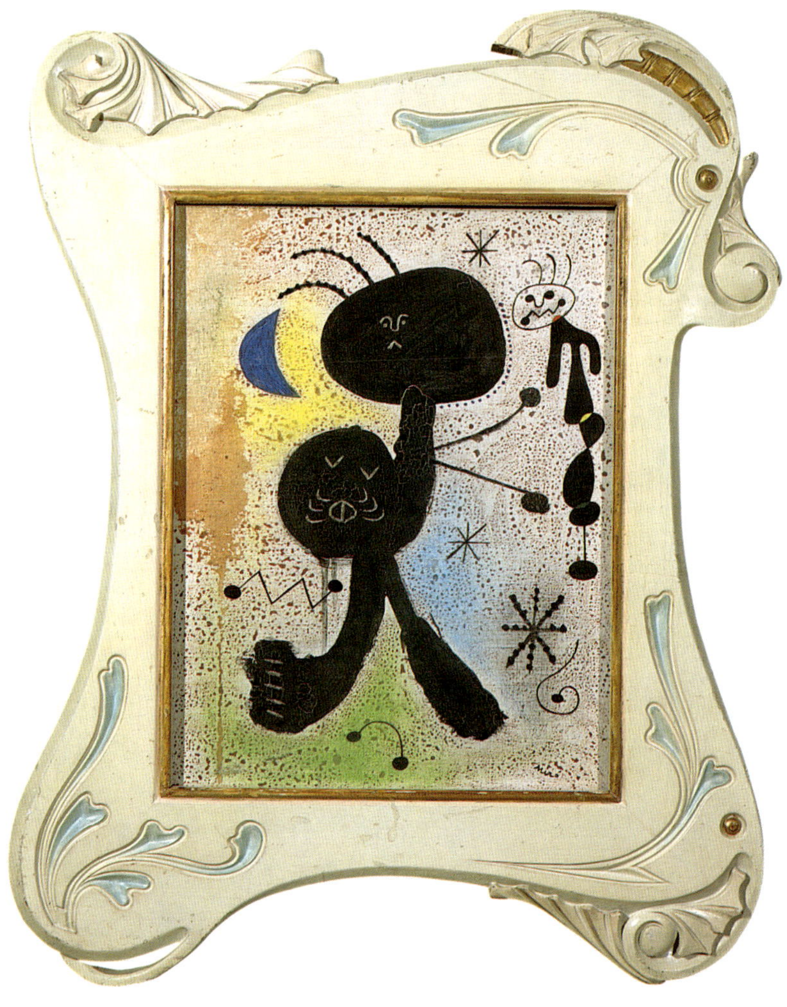

The diamond smiles at twilight,
1947. On permanent loan from
Emili Fernández i Miró

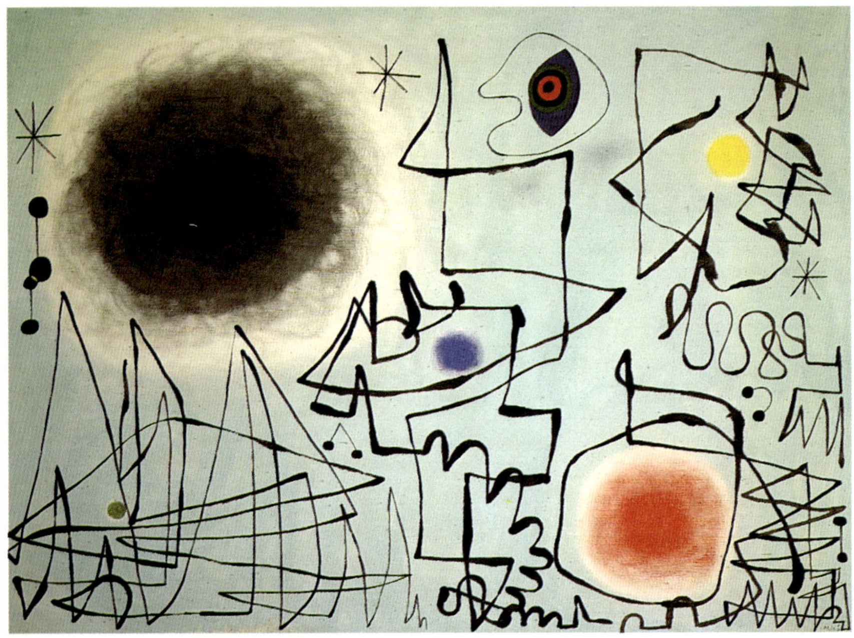

Painting, 1954. Gift of Joan Prats

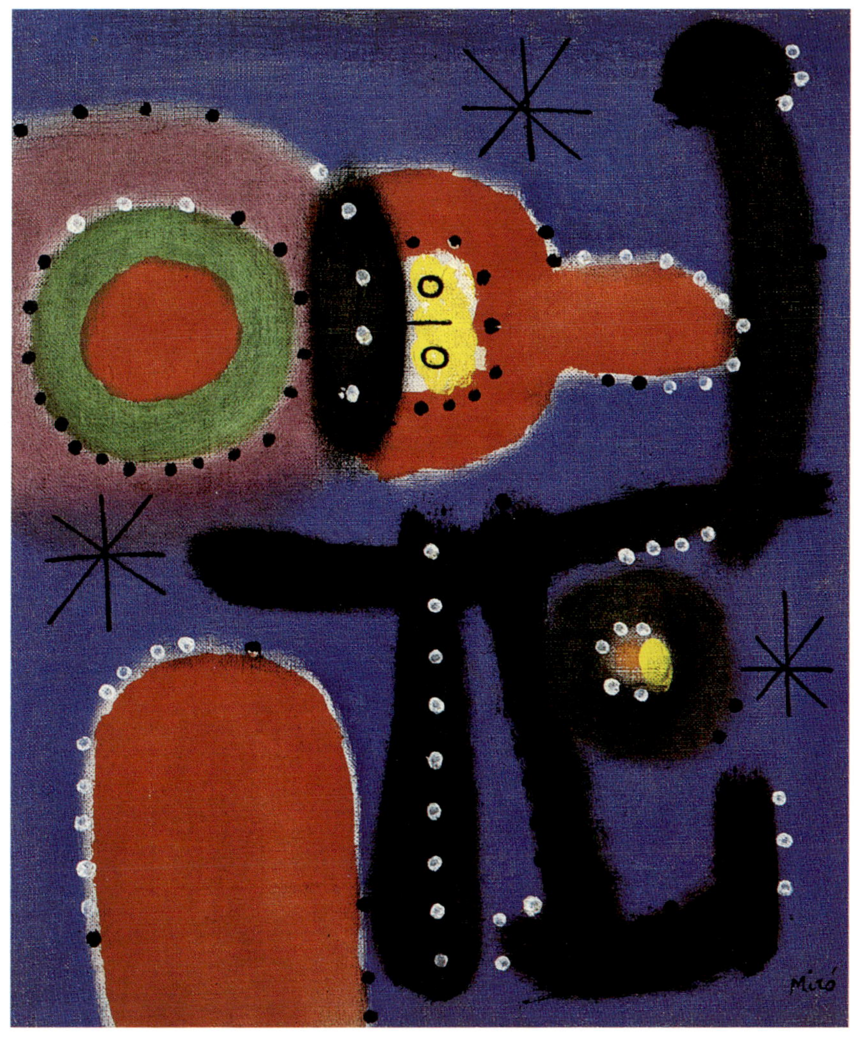

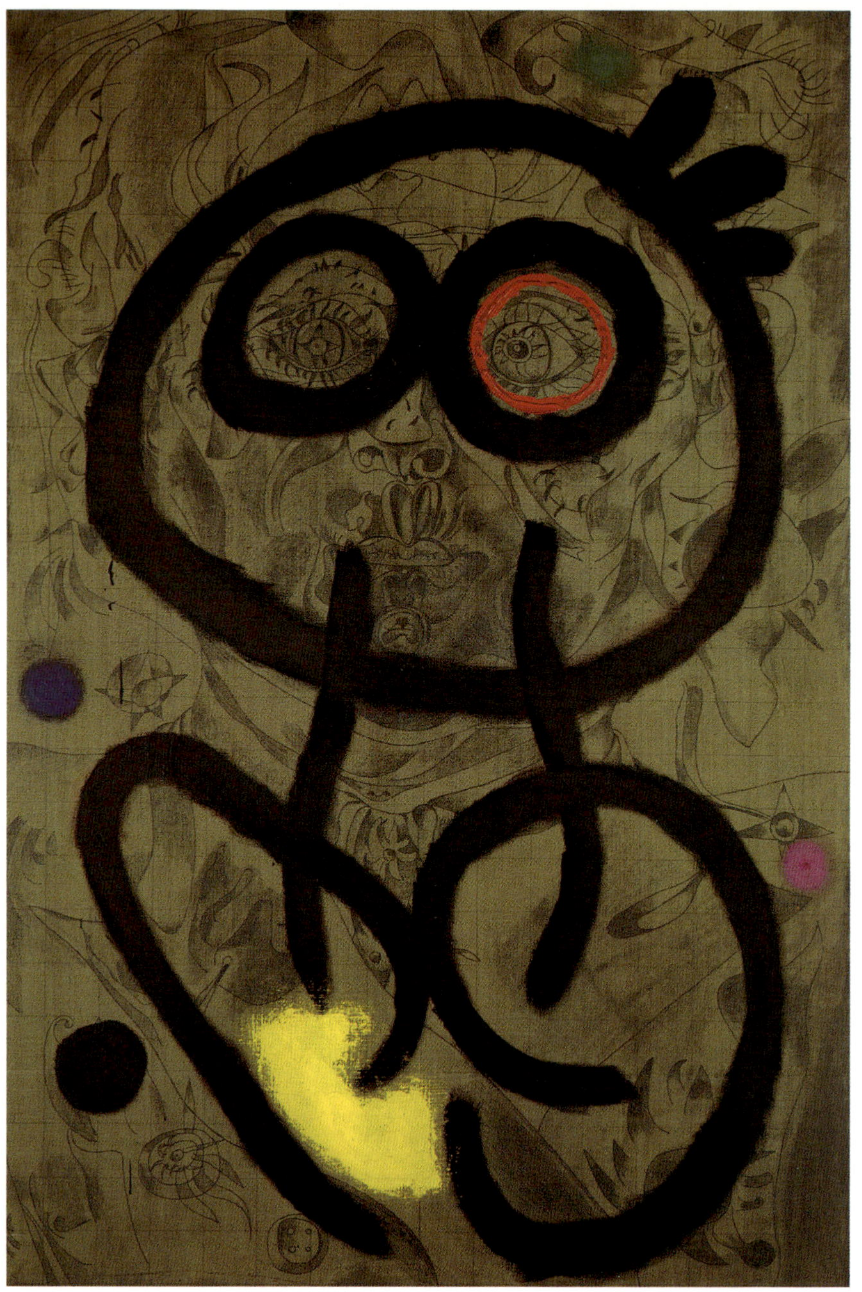

Self-portrait, 1937-38/1960. On permanent loan from Maria Dolors Miró

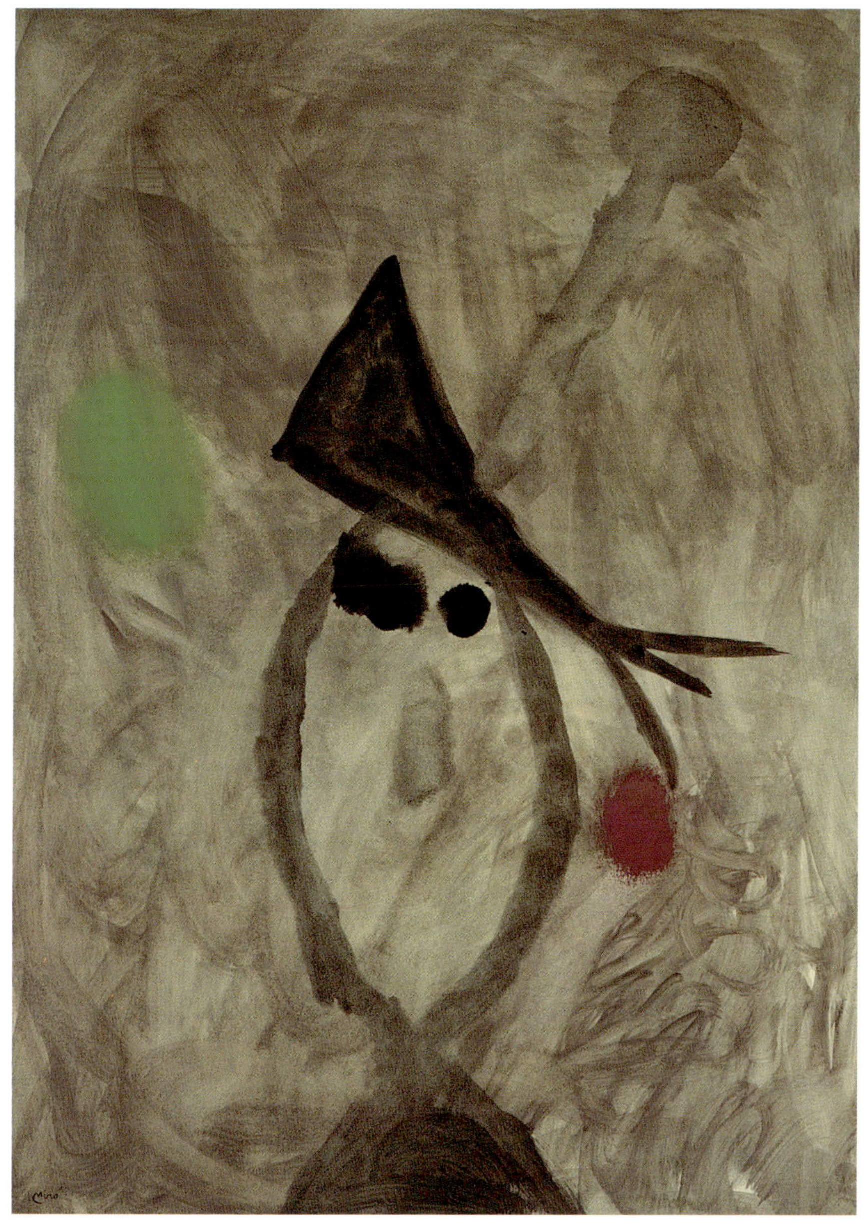

Woman in a pretty hat,
1960

Taking Miró's work as a whole, as the product of a lifetime of exploration and experiment coupled with strict self-criticism, we can see that the early paintings are characterised by their precision and attention to detail, and those of the later period by direct, decisive strokes and a spontaneity in the act of painting: blobs of colour, dribbles of paint, brush marks and even the imprint of the hand.

During the last twenty years of his life, Miró diversified his experiments with other techniques. In 1966 he began working regularly on bronze sculpture. As in the forties, the procedure used in most instances was the *cire perdue* method, but he made less use of modelling and preferred to assemble a variety of everyday bits and pieces that, when cast in bronze, almost always coalesced into biomorphic beings. Working with different foundries (Parellada, Clémenti, Susse, Scuderi and Bonvicini) produced different patinas on the sculptures. In the mid-1960s Miró also experimented with the application of colour to a number of these pieces.

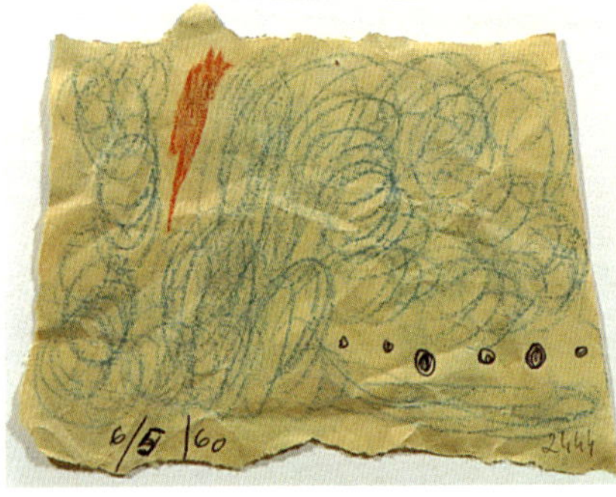

Preliminary sketch for *Blue II*, 1961

Sculpture also allowed him to produce works for different public places – in his own words, "a collective art" to be enjoyed by everyone, which always interested him. This was the case with the monumental sculptures *Couple playing with almond blossom* (1975) for the district of La Défense in Paris, and *Woman and bird* (1982) for the Parc de Joan Miró in Barcelona.

Miró began working on ceramics in 1944 with his friend the ceramicist Josep Llorens i Artigas. After an initial phase from 1944 to 1947, when he learned the techniques of firing and glazing, his so-called ceramic period commenced around 1954-56. The Foundation has one piece from this time, when Miró was experimenting with various types of clay and the formulae for obtaining colours: *Double-sided stele* dated 1956.

Two years later, in 1958, Miró and Artigas embarked on large ceramic murals, producing the *Wall of the sun* and *Wall of the moon* for the UNESCO headquarters in Paris. In 1960 they made a mural for Harvard University, and between 1964 and 1972 received commissions for five more: for the Handelshochschule in St. Gallen, Switzerland (1964), the Solomon R. Guggenheim Museum, New York (1966), Barcelona Airport (1970), the Kunsthaus in Zurich (1971) and the Cinémathèque in Paris (1972). The Foundation holds the documentation relating to two of these – the Guggenheim Museum and Barcelona Airport – the former consisting of maquettes and notes that Miró used for the mural *Alicia,* and the latter consisting of the initial maquette.

After the death of Josep Llorens i Artigas, his son Joan Gardy Artigas continued working with Miró. Together they made the ceramic paving for the Pla de l'Os in the Rambla in Barcelona, and the maquette for this is also held at the Foundation.

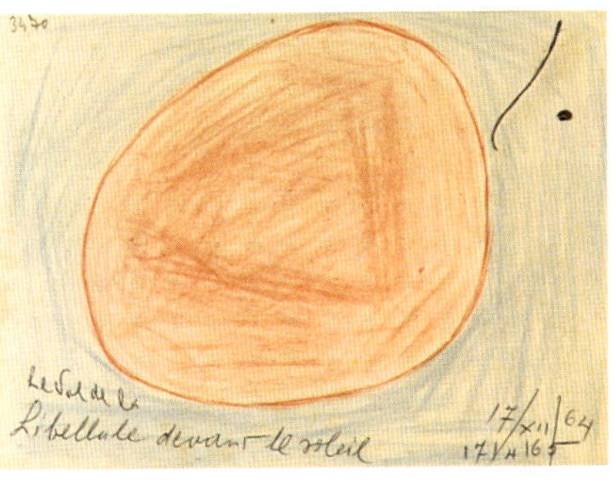

Preliminary sketch for *Flight of the dragonfly in front of the sun,* 1968

In 1972, Miró produced his first textiles – which can be placed somewhere between painting, collage and tapestry – in the form of *sobreteixims* and sacks.

The starting point for the *sobreteixims* was the neutral tapestry base prepared by Josep Royo with rustic materials such as jute, hemp, esparto grass and twine. Onto this, Miró poured petrol and let the flames take over, so that chance played its part. He then applied the colour, either with paint, appliquéd felt or skeins of wool.

Miró also used fire again in 1973 to produce the series of "burnt canvases" (three of which are held by the Foundation) that seem an attempt to show his scepticism for the concept of works of art.

In 1974, his work with textiles took a new turn after he received a commission to make a large-format tapestry for the foyer of a New York skyscraper. In 1977, the National Gallery of Art in Washington D.C. asked him for one of much the same type, measuring 11 x 7 metres. On completing it, Miró decided to produce a large tapestry very similar in concept to the Washington one, which he donated to the Foundation in 1979.

For Emili, 1963. On permanent loan from Emili Fernández i Miró

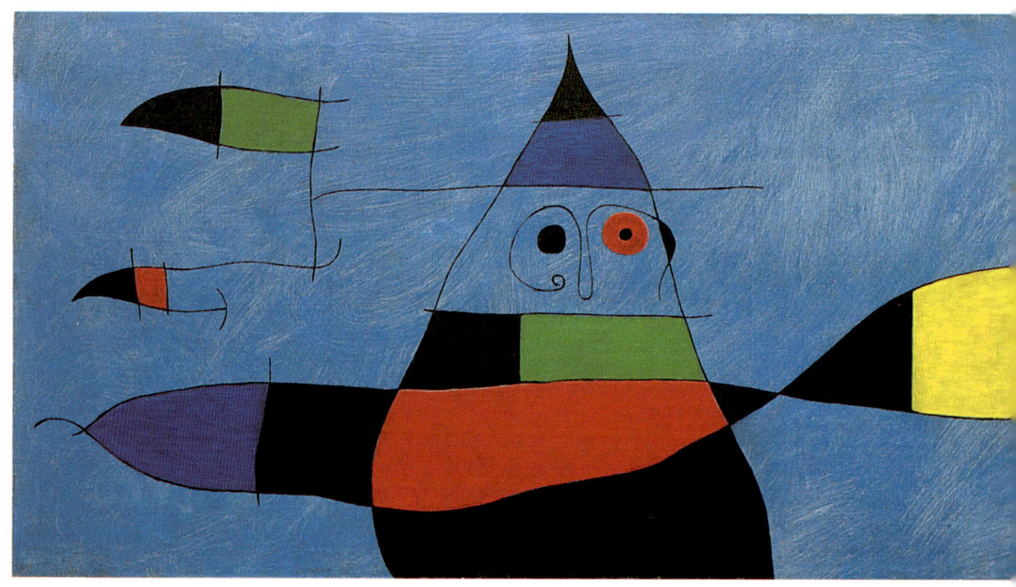

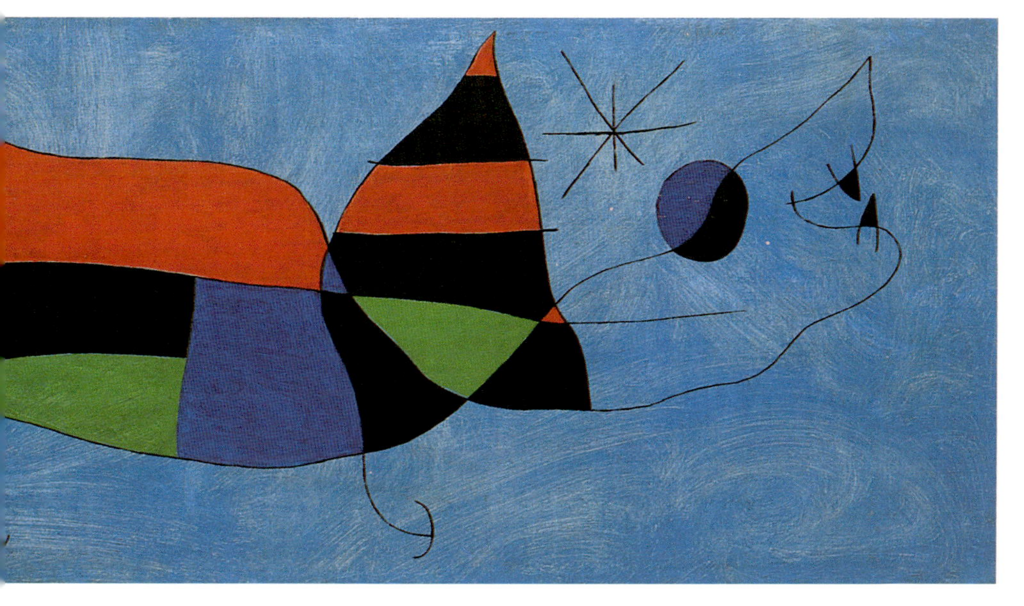

Figure in front of the sun, 1968

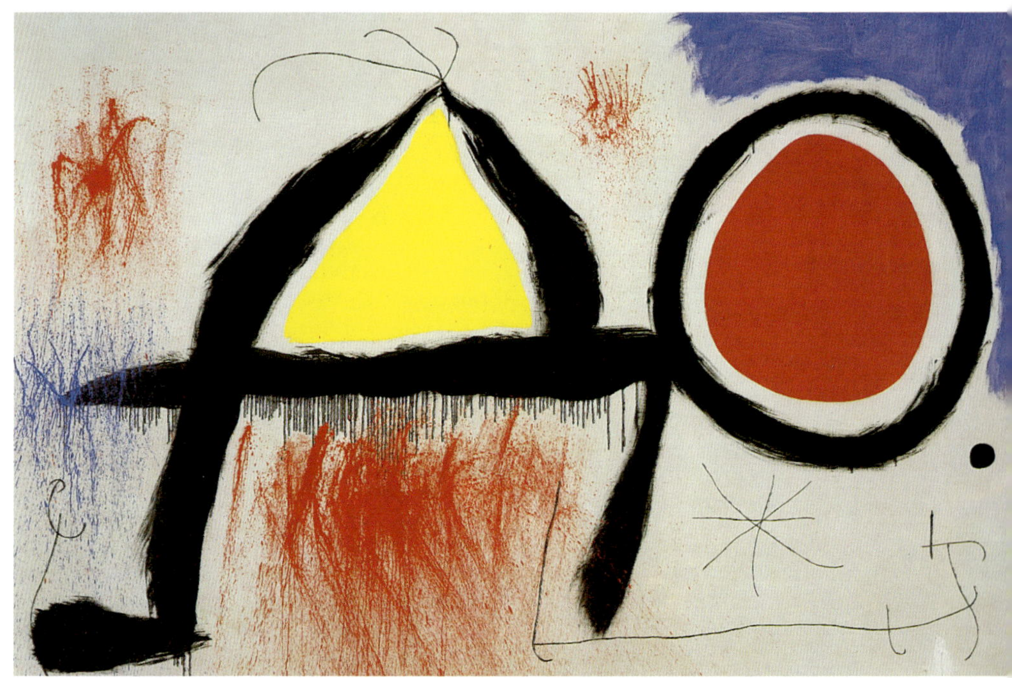

Catalan peasant in the moonlight, 1968

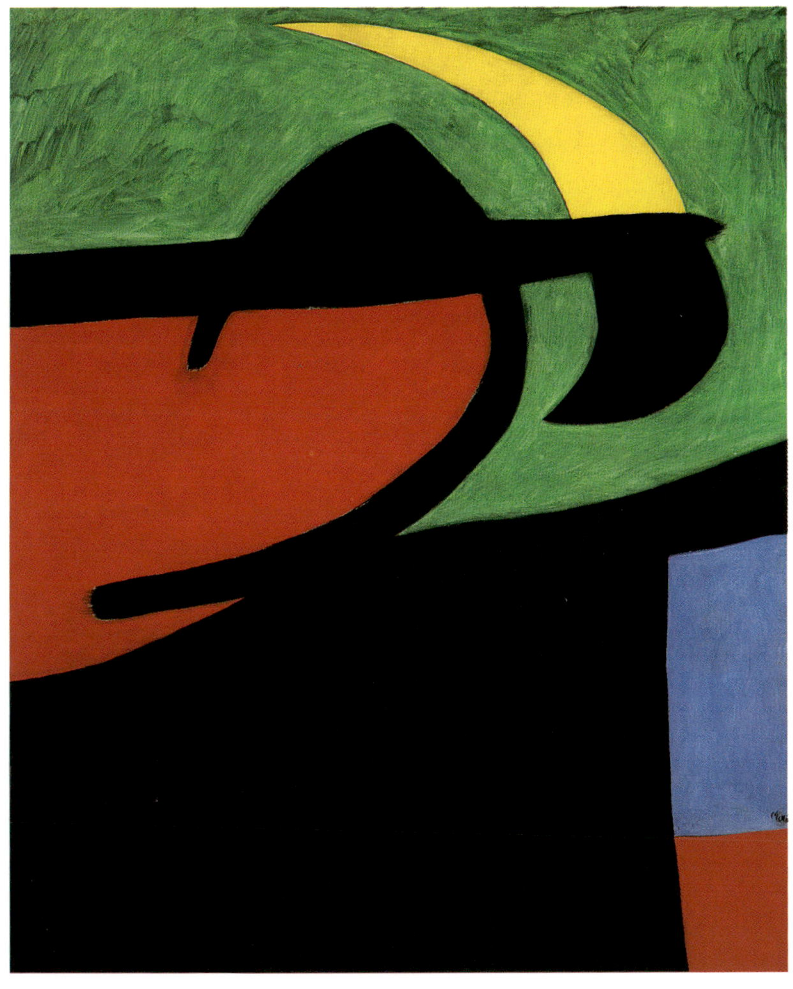

Among the "Miró papers", the Foundation has a copy of Alfred Jarry's *Ubu Roi*, published in Paris in 1921. In the margins and on small scraps of paper originally placed inside the book are a number of drawings by Miró closely connected with the text. From the nature of these drawings they can be presumed to pre-date the publication in 1966 of a special limited edition of *Ubu Roi* for which Miró produced thirteen lithographs. Other related pieces that have survived from the same period are detailed illustrations for *Ubu Roi*, which were never published but which show a faithful relationship between text and image that can almost be read like a story in pictures.

Miró was fascinated with Ubu, a grotesque figure whose bodily functions predominate over his intellectual ones, and kept the subject constantly in mind. This creature that was a caricature of all that is despicable in the human being appeared in two further limited-edition books, *Ubu aux Baléares*, 1973 and *L'enfance d'Ubu*, 1975 – the first with illustrations and text by Miró, the second with illustrations by Miró and texts taken from somewhat vulgar Majorcan and Catalan sayings.

It was this material, donated by Miró to the Foundation, that was used by the members of the Teatre de la Claca group in order to give shape and volume to the giant puppet figures for the spectacle *Mori el Merma* performed in 1978. Miró brought life to the figures by painting them. These puppets, Miró's last great creative work, now form part of the Foundation's collections.

In June 1975, as already mentioned, the Joan Miró Foundation was opened to the public. Miró made a major donation of works at that time, and the following year he gave the Foundation practically the entire collection of "Miró papers". He subsequently made further donations of paintings on various supports as well as sketchbooks.

Thanks to the existence of all these items, to the orderly way in which Miró worked and to his immense generosity, we have been able to make this documentary material accessible to students, academics and anyone else interested in following Miró's artistic career from its early beginnings to his last years. It is one of the most exciting adventures in twentieth-century art.

Lovers playing with almond blossom, 1975. Maquette for the sculptural group at La Défense (Paris)

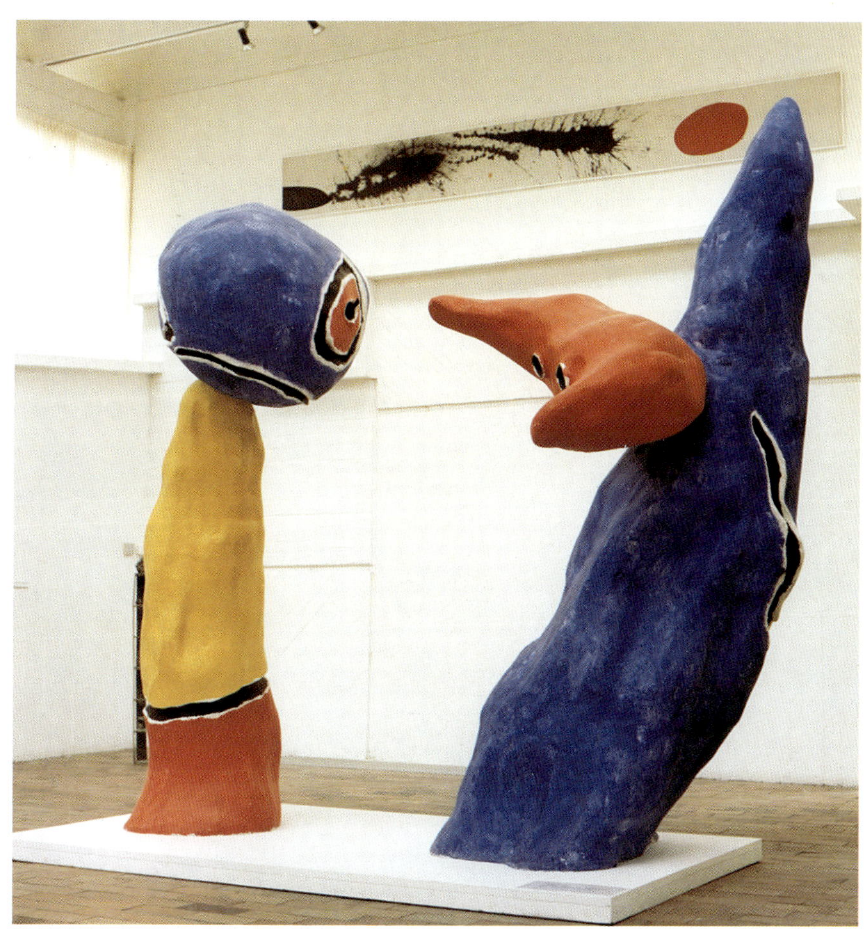

The bird makes its nest in the fingers in flower, 1969

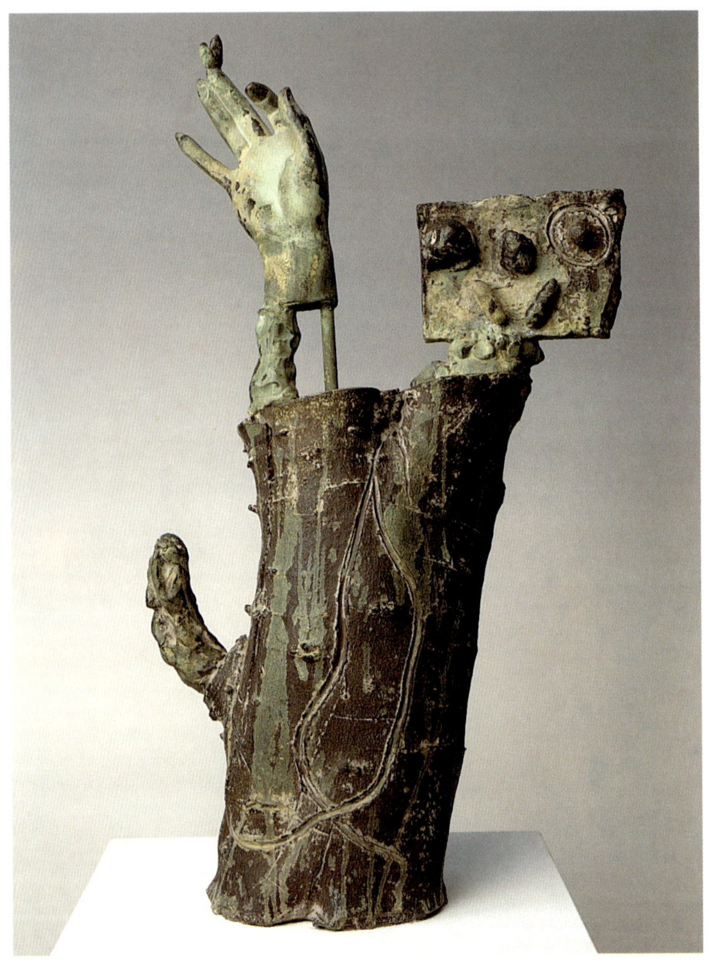

Maquette for the ceramic mural
at Barcelona Airport, 1970

Ubu Roi, undated

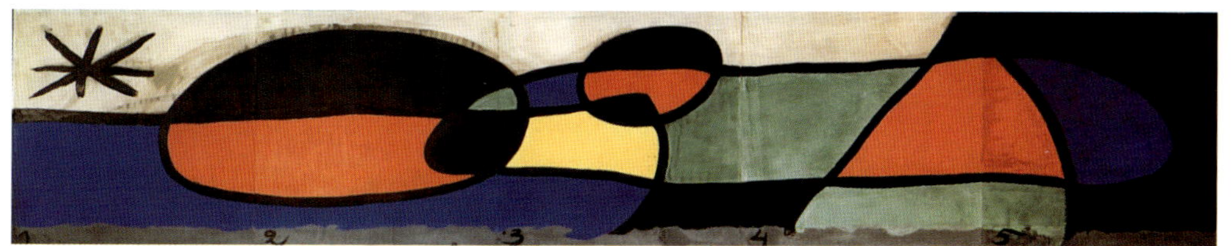

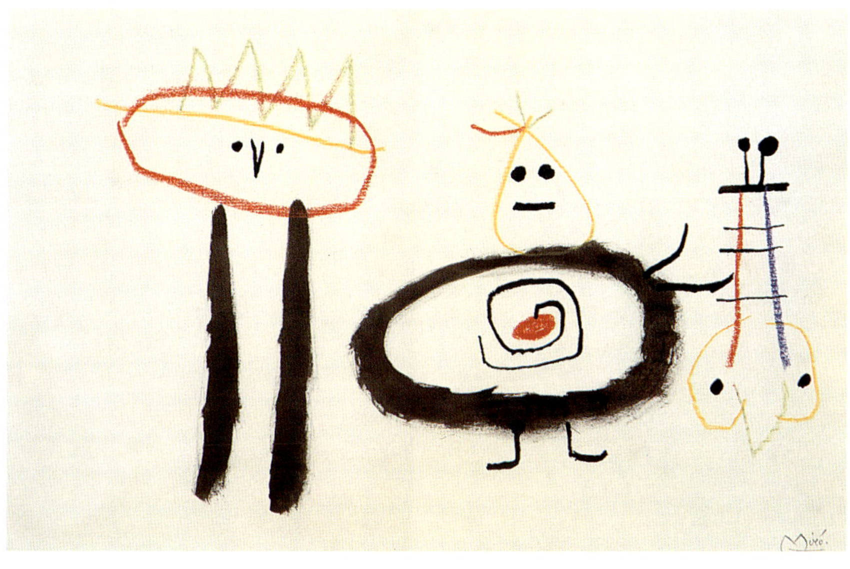

Double-sided stele, 1956.
Gift of Galerie Lelong

Tapestry of the Foundation,
1979

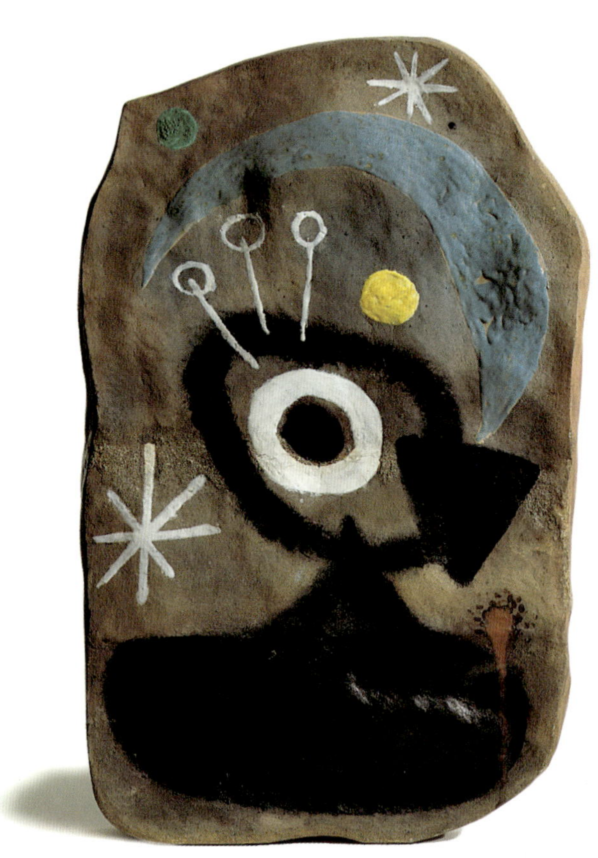

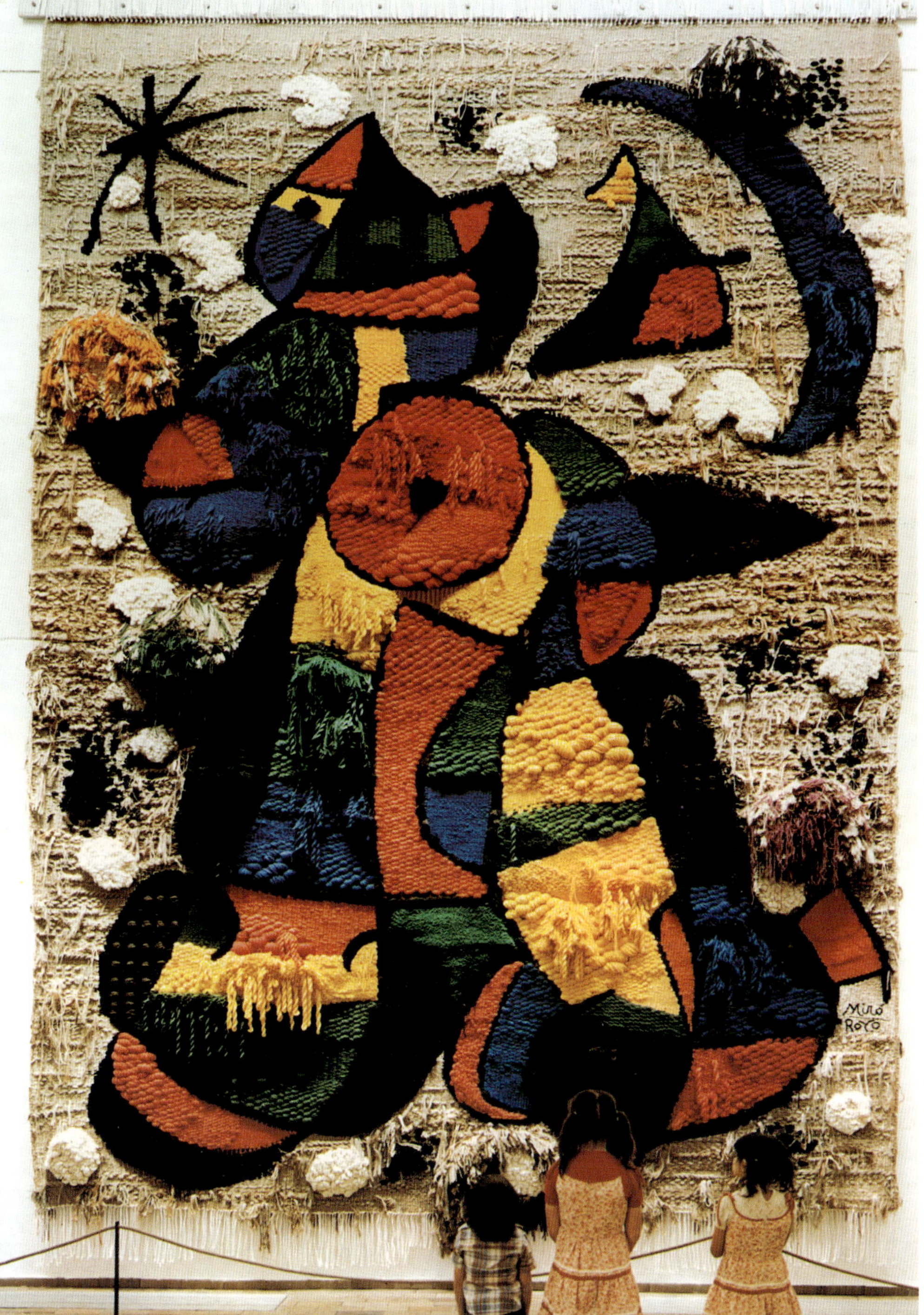
Miró
Royo

Ceramic paving in the Pla de l'Os, 1976

Birds of the caves II, 1971. On permanent loan from Joan Punyet i Miró

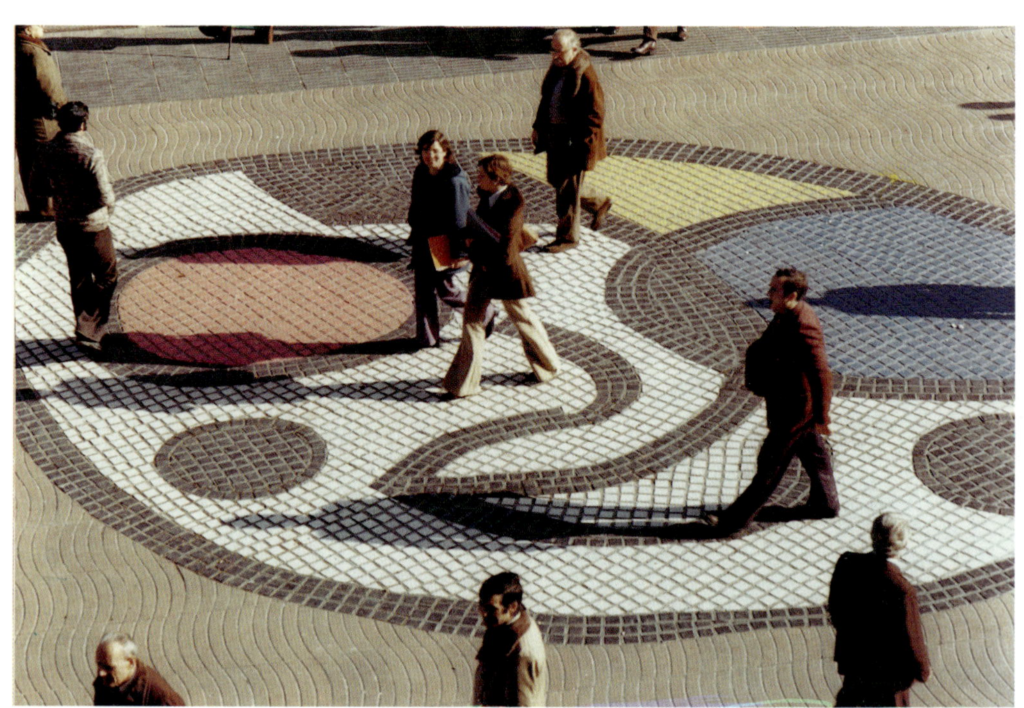

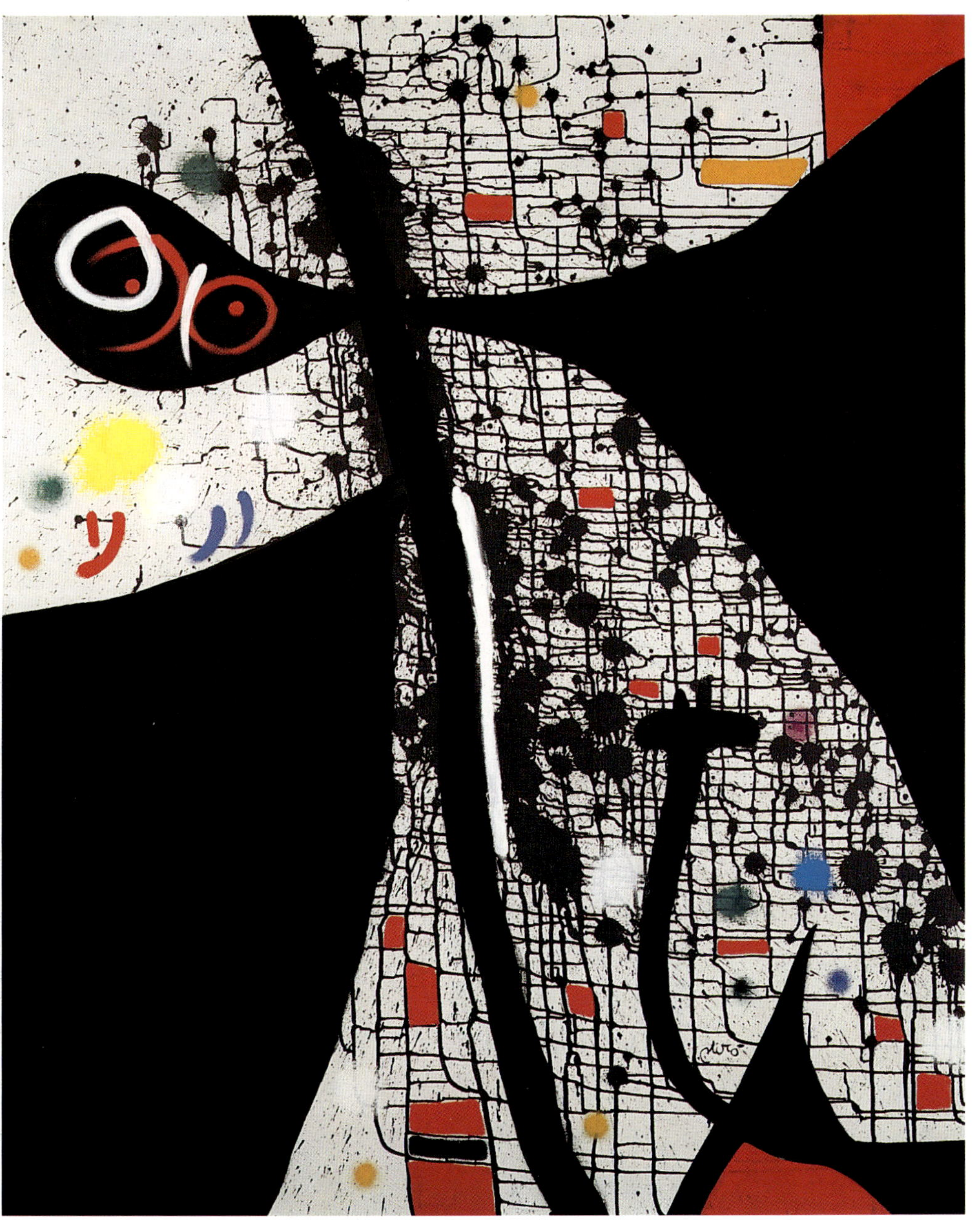

The hope of the man condemned to death I, II, III,
1974

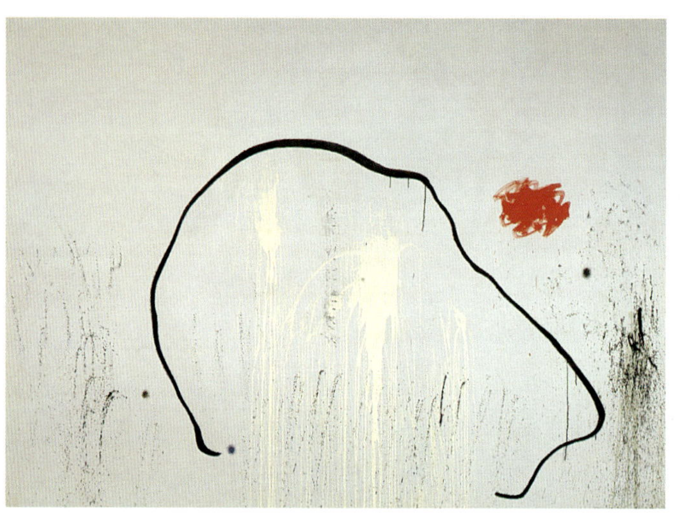

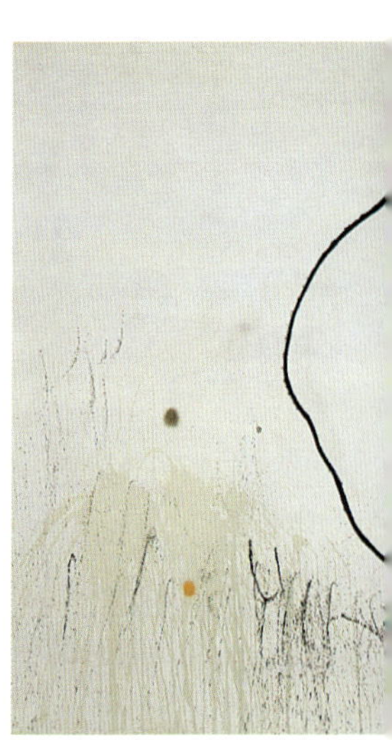

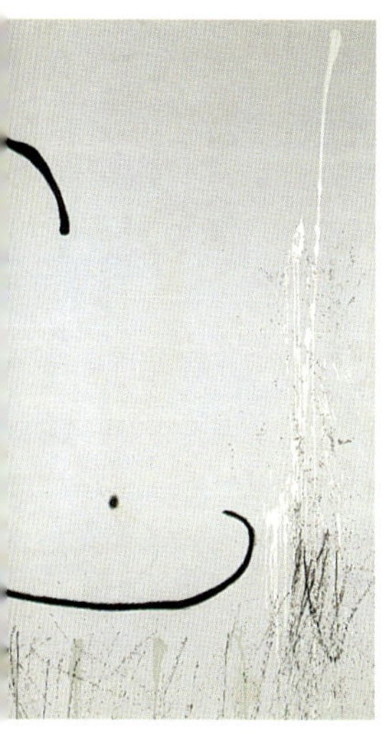

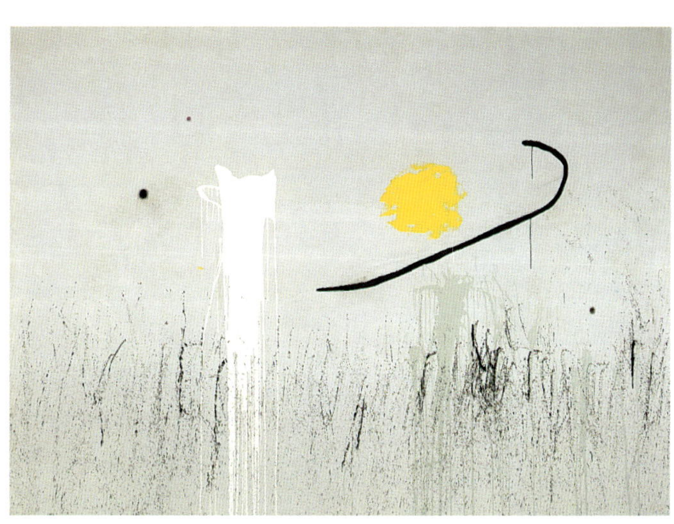

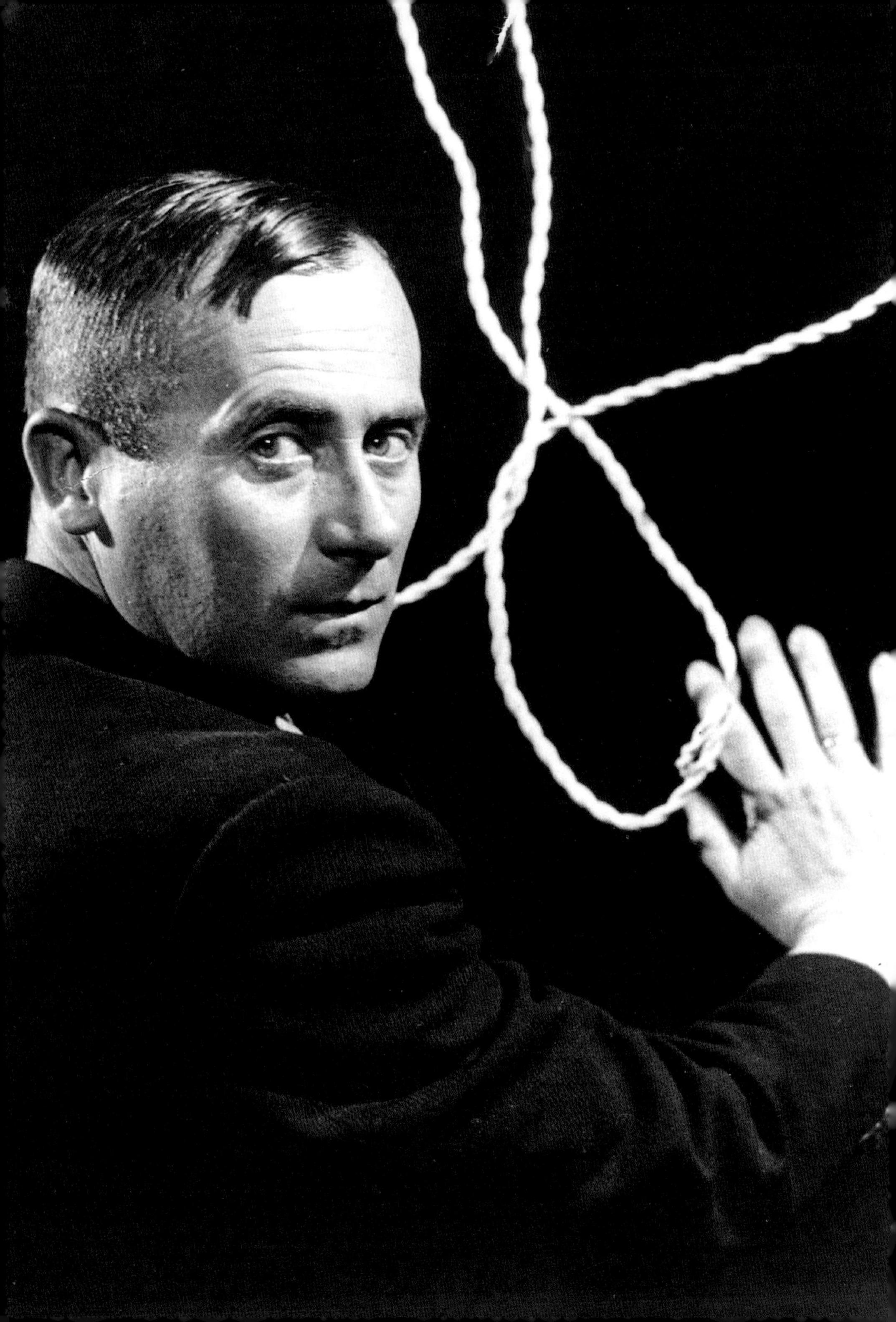

Chronology

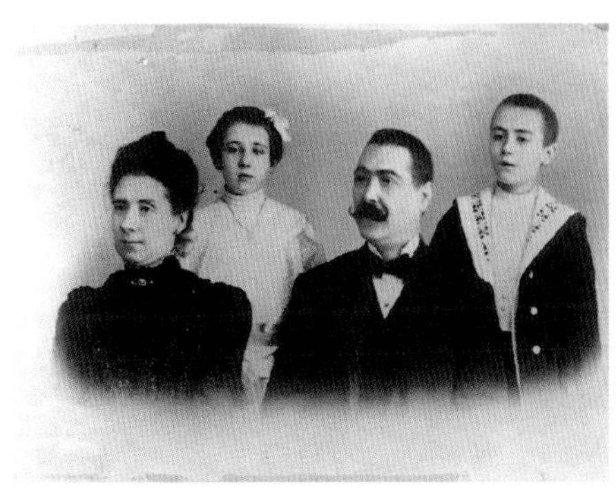

Joan Miró with his parents and sister Dolors

1893
20 April: Birth of Joan Miró i Ferrà at 9.00 p.m. at number 4 Passatge del Crèdit, Barcelona. His father, Miquel Miró i Adzerias, son of a blacksmith in Cornudella, was a watchmaker and silversmith. His mother, Dolors Ferrà i Oromí, was the daughter of a cabinet-maker in Palma, Majorca.

1900
Begins primary school at Carrer del Regomir 13, Barcelona, where he attends drawing classes given by Sr. Civil.

1901
The earliest preserved drawings, now at the Joan Miró Foundation in Barcelona, date from this year.

1907
Enrols at the School of Commerce in Barcelona. At the same time he attends classes at the School of Industrial and Fine Arts (the Llotja) until 1910, where his teachers are Modest Urgell and Josep Pascó.

1910
Works as an accounts clerk at Dalmau i Oliveres drugstore in Barcelona.
Participates for the first time at an exhibition of old and modern portraits and drawings organised by the City Council.

1911
His inability to adapt to the job at Dalmau i Oliveres affects his health. He catches typhoid fever and spends time convalescing in Mont-roig (province of Tarragona) at the farm recently bought by his parents.

1912
Decides to devote himself entirely to painting and enrols in the school of art run by Francesc Galí, which he attends until 1915. Among his fellow students are Joan Prats, Josep Francesc Ràfols, Enric Cristòfol Ricart and possibly Josep Llorens Artigas, among others.

1913
Enrols in the Cercle Artístic de Sant Lluc, where he attends life classes. Here he meets up again with Joan Prats, with whom he forms a close friendship.

1916
Meets the dealer Josep Dalmau, who shows an interest in his work. Rents a studio with E.C. Ricart in Carrer de Sant Pere més Baix 51,

Joan Miró photographed by Man Ray, Paris, 1933

Joan Miró and other students from Francesc Galí's art school on the beach in Barcelona, 1912-15

Joan Miró in his Barcelona studio, 1918-1920

Joan Miró and Pilar Juncosa on their wedding day. Palma, 12 October 1929

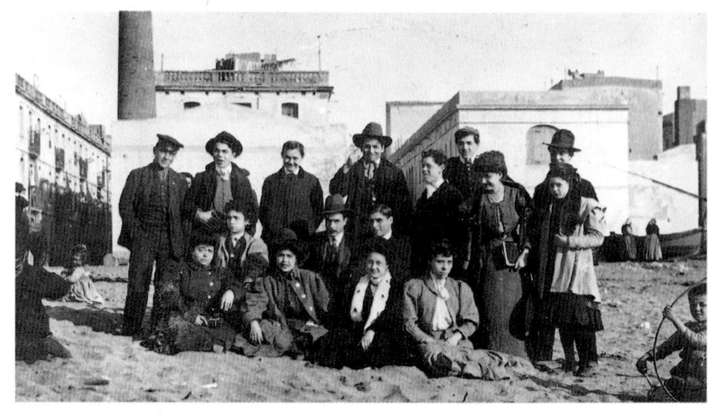

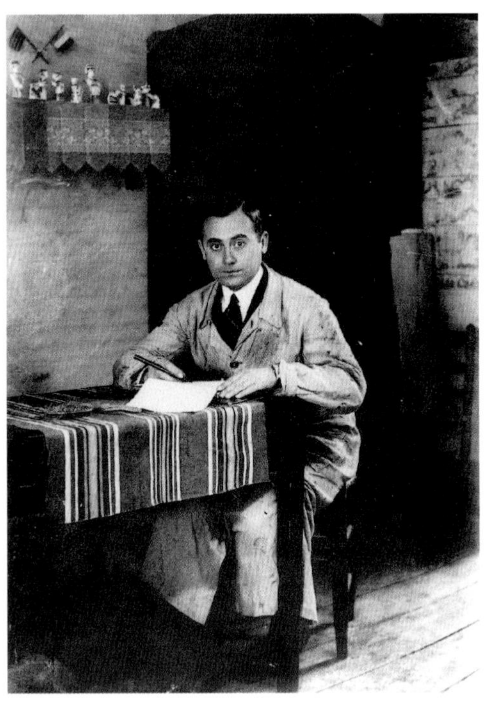

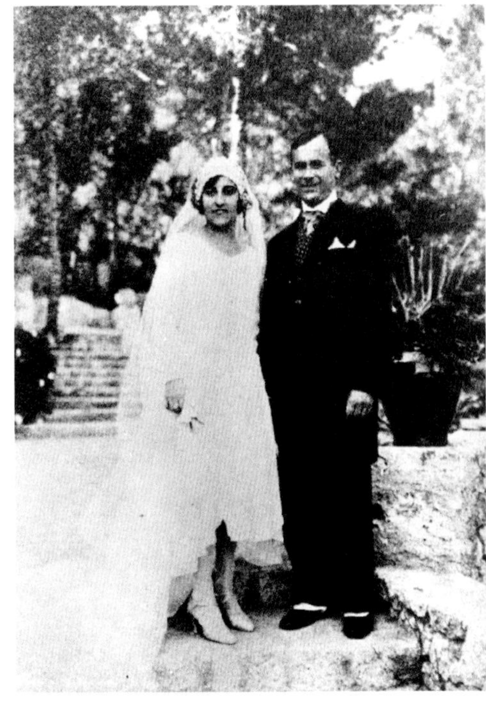

Barcelona, which they share until 1918.

1917

Through Josep Dalmau he probably meets Maurice Raynal and Francis Picabia.

Takes an interest in poetry and reads Catalan and French avant-garde reviews such as Pierre Reverdy's *Nord-Sud* and Albert Birot's *SIC*.

Visits the "Exposition d'Art Français" in Barcelona.

1918

Forms part of the Agrupació Courbet together with Josep Llorens Artigas, J.F. Ràfols, E.C. Ricart, Rafael Sala, Francesc Domingo and Marià Espinal, all students of Galí's art school and the Cercle Artístic de Sant Lluc.

First one-man show at the Galeries Dalmau, Barcelona.

1920

Travels to Paris for the first time, where Josep Dalmau tries to organise an exhibition for him. Visits Picasso in his studio.

1921

In Paris until 1925, where he has the use of Pablo Gargallo's studio at 45 Rue Blomet during the academic terms. Spends the rest of the year mainly at Mont-roig.

First solo exhibition in Paris at the Galerie La Licorne, organised by Josep Dalmau. The introduction to the catalogue is written by Maurice Raynal.

1922

In Paris, living and working at 45 Rue Blomet. Becomes friendly with André Masson, who is a neighbour, and with Roland Tual.

1923

Through Masson he meets Michel Leiris and probably Antonin Artaud, Robert Desnos, Jean Dubuffet, Paul Éluard, Marcel Jouhandeau, Georges Limbour, Raymond Queneau and Armand Salacrou. He also meets Ernest Hemingway, who purchases *The farm*, and Ezra Pound.

In Mont-roig he begins painting *Tilled field, Catalan landscape (The hunter)* and *Pastoral*, which mark a turning point in his art.

1924

Avant-garde poets and writers gather in Masson's studio at 45 Rue Blomet. Miró's friends during this period are Max Jacob, Michel Leiris, Georges Limbour, Benjamin Péret, Armand Salacrou and Roland Tual.

1925

André Breton meets Miró during a visit to the studio in the Rue Blomet.

First solo exhibition at the Galerie Pierre, Paris.

1926

Moves into a new studio at 22 Rue Tourlaque, in the Cité des Fusains. His neighbours are Max Ernst, Hans Arp and probably Paul Éluard and Camille Goemans.

Diaghilev commissions Miró and Ernst to design the sets and costumes for the ballet *Romeo and Juliet* to be performed by the Ballets Russes.

1928

Produces the first object-collages titled *Spanish dancer*.

Visits Belgium and Holland.

Paints the *Dutch interiors* in Mont-roig.

1929

Works on the series known as "Imaginary portraits".

Marries Pilar Juncosa in Palma, Majorca. They settle in Paris, in an apartment at 3 Rue François Mouton.

1930

Works on a series of paintings in very varied styles. According to Miró, they are a farewell to painting, albeit a temporary one, as he wishes to work in other media such as bas relief, sculpture, etc.

Birth of his only daughter, Maria Dolors, in Barcelona.

In Mont-roig he produces his first three-dimensional pieces.

First one-man show in the United States, at the Valentine Gallery, New York.

1931

In Mont-roig he starts a series of paintings on Ingres paper and object-paintings.

1932

Through Joan Prats he meets the architect Josep Lluís Sert.

Decides to spend more time in Barcelona. Lives and works in the family home at Passatge del Crèdit 4 until 1936.

Works on a new series of objects.

Designs the curtain, sets, costumes and objects for the ballet *Jeux d'enfants* performed by the Ballets Russes de Montecarlo, with scenario by Boris Kochno, music by Georges Bizet and choreography by Léonide Massine.

First one-man show at the Pierre Matisse Gallery, New York.

1933

Works on a series of 18 collages and then on the paintings based on them.

Publication of *Enfance*s by Georges Hugnet, the first book illustrated by Miró with etchings.

1934

Signs a contract with Pierre Matisse, who represents him in the United States.

1936

Starts a series of 27 paintings on masonite.

Travels to Paris with his latest works, which are to be exhibited in New York. Due to the outbreak of the Spanish Civil War, he decides to stay in Paris. His wife and daughter join him, and they remain in France until 1940.

1937

Living and working in an apartment at 98 Boulevard Auguste Blanqui, Paris.

Attends life classes at the Académie de la Grande Chaumière, where he produces a large number of drawings.

Produces a large mural painting, *The reaper (Catalan peasant in revolt)*, for the Spanish Republican Government's pavilion, designed by Josep Lluís Sert and Luis Lacasa, at the Paris World Fair.

1938

Works on etchings and dry-point engravings with Marcoussis and prints these at the studios of Roger Lacourière and Stanley W. Hayter.

1939

Leaves Paris in the summer and rents a house in Varengeville-sur-Mer, Normandy, where the family remain until 1940.

1940

In January he starts a series of 23 gouaches, which he continues in Palma and completes in Mont-roig in September 1941. This series was later to be known as the *Constellations*.

The Germans bomb Normandy at the end of May and Miró decides to return to Spain with his family, where they settle in Palma (Majorca).

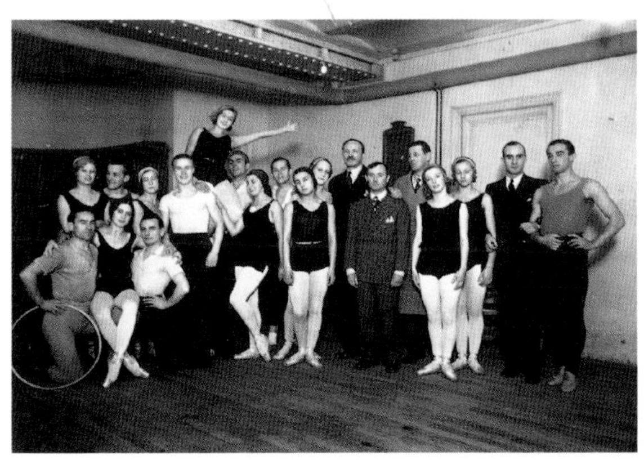

Joan Miró with the Ballets Russes de Montecarlo, 1932

Joan Miró painting *The reaper* in the Spanish Republican Government's pavilion at the Paris World Fair, 1937

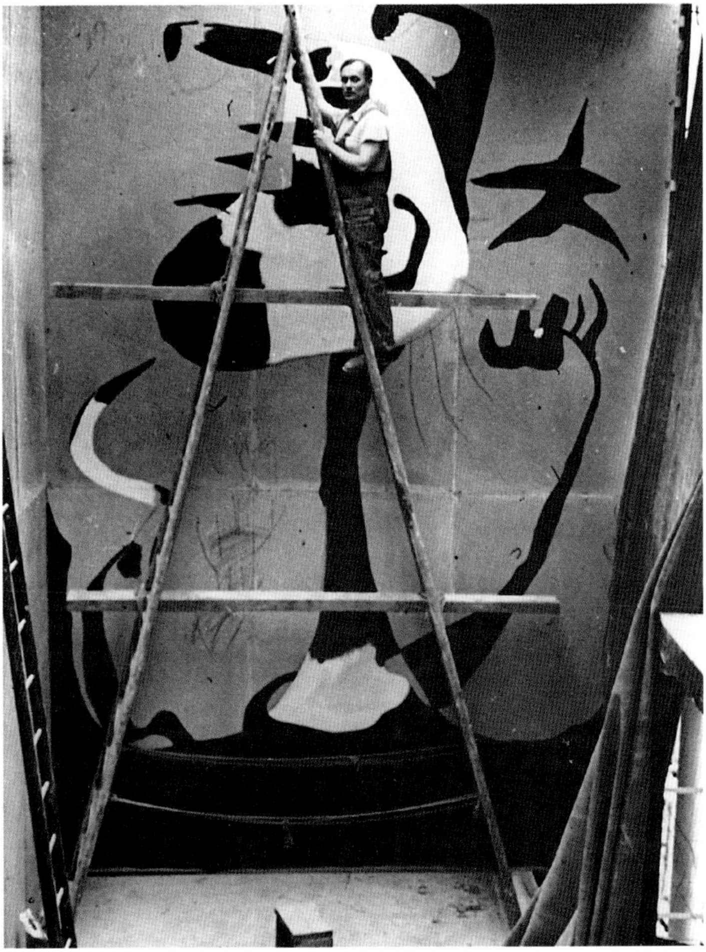

Joan Miró with Joan Prats during production of the *Barcelona series*, Barcelona, May 1944

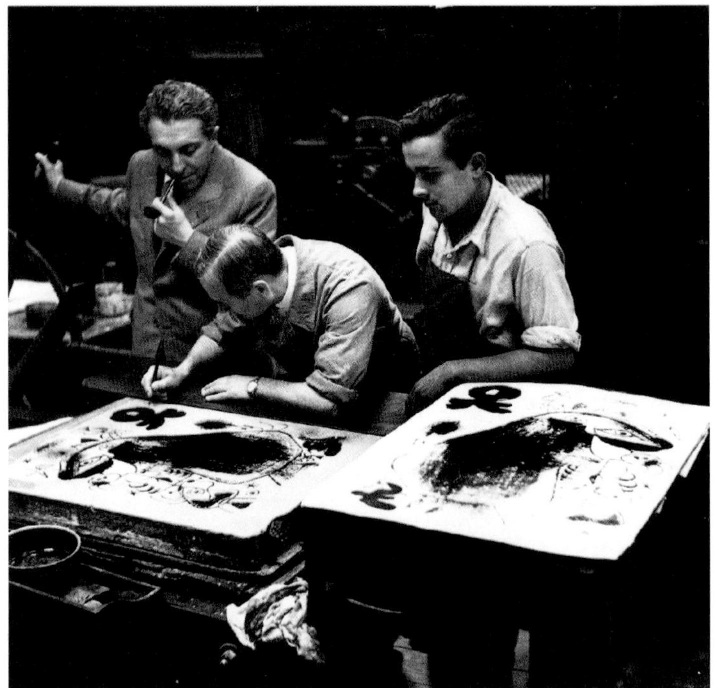

1941

First large retrospective exhibition at the Museum of Modern Art, New York. Organisation and catalogue by James Johnson Sweeney.

1942

Continues working exclusively on paper.

Returns to Barcelona and lives at Passatge del Crèdit 4.

1943

Continues working exclusively on paper, with the sole known exception of *Painting with art nouveau frame,* from the Joan Prats collection.

1944

Produces his first ceramics, using materials from an unsuccessful firing in 1941 by Josep Llorens Artigas. This is the start of the first period of collaboration between them, which continues until 1947.

Publication of the set of 50 lithographs known as the *Barcelona series*, under the supervision of Joan Prats.

Returns to painting on canvas, which he had virtually abandoned since 1939.

1945

Works on several series of large-format paintings.

1946

Produces his first bronze sculptures.

1947

First trip to the United States, where he produces a mural painting for the Gourmet Room at the Terrace Plaza Hotel in Cincinnati.

During his stay in New York he frequents Stanley W. Hayter's studio Atelier 17, where he experiments with engraving techniques.

Takes part in "Le Surréalisme en 1947: Exposition internationale du

Joan Miró and Josep Llorens Artigas working on ceramics, Gallifa, 1954-56

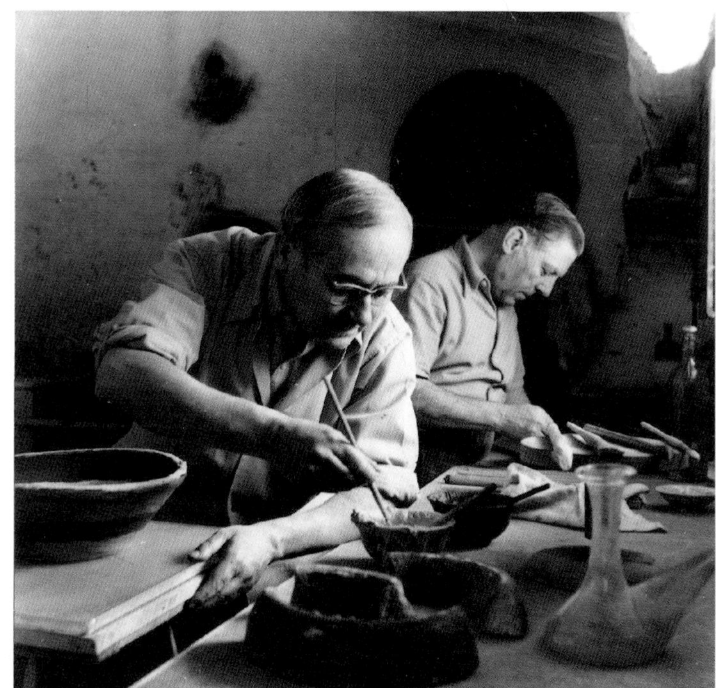

Following pages:

Joan Miró working in the studio designed for him by Josep Lluís Sert in Palma, Majorca, 1962

surréalisme" at the Galerie Maeght, Paris, organised by André Breton and Marcel Duchamp.

1948

First solo exhibition at the Galerie Maeght, Paris. Aimé Maeght becomes his new representative in France.

1949

This year and next he alternates between two types of painting: one more reflective and the other more gestural and impulsive.

Although based in Barcelona, he makes frequent visits to Paris to work on printing techniques at the Mourlot printing studio (lithographs) and at the Atelier Lacourière (engravings). His work on ceramics and sculpture becomes increasingly intensive.

Exhibition at the Galerías Layetanas, Barcelona, sponsored by Cobalto 49.

1950

In Barcelona, living and working at Passatge del Crèdit 4 until the autumn, when he moves to a flat at Carrer de Folgaroles 9, where he also works, although he keeps on the studio in the Passatge del Crèdit.

Starts work on the mural painting for the dining hall at Harkness Commons, Harvard University, commissioned by Walter Gropius, which he completes the following year.

1951

In Mont-roig, working on sculptures in a studio he had built at the farm.

1952

Second visit to the United States.

1954

Starts a new period of collaboration with Josep Llorens Artigas in Gallifa (near Barcelona). Over the next two years he produces more than 200 ceramic pieces.

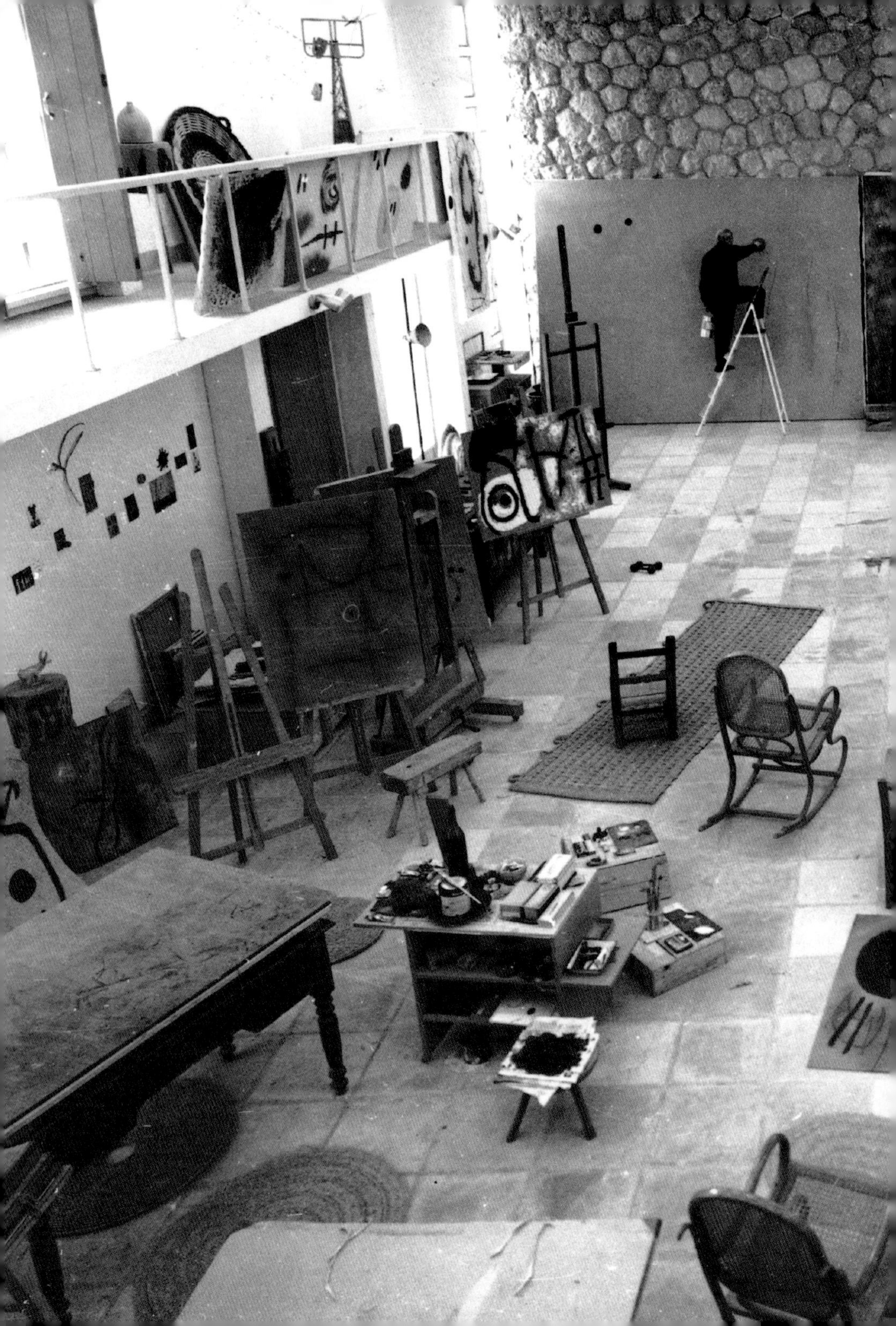

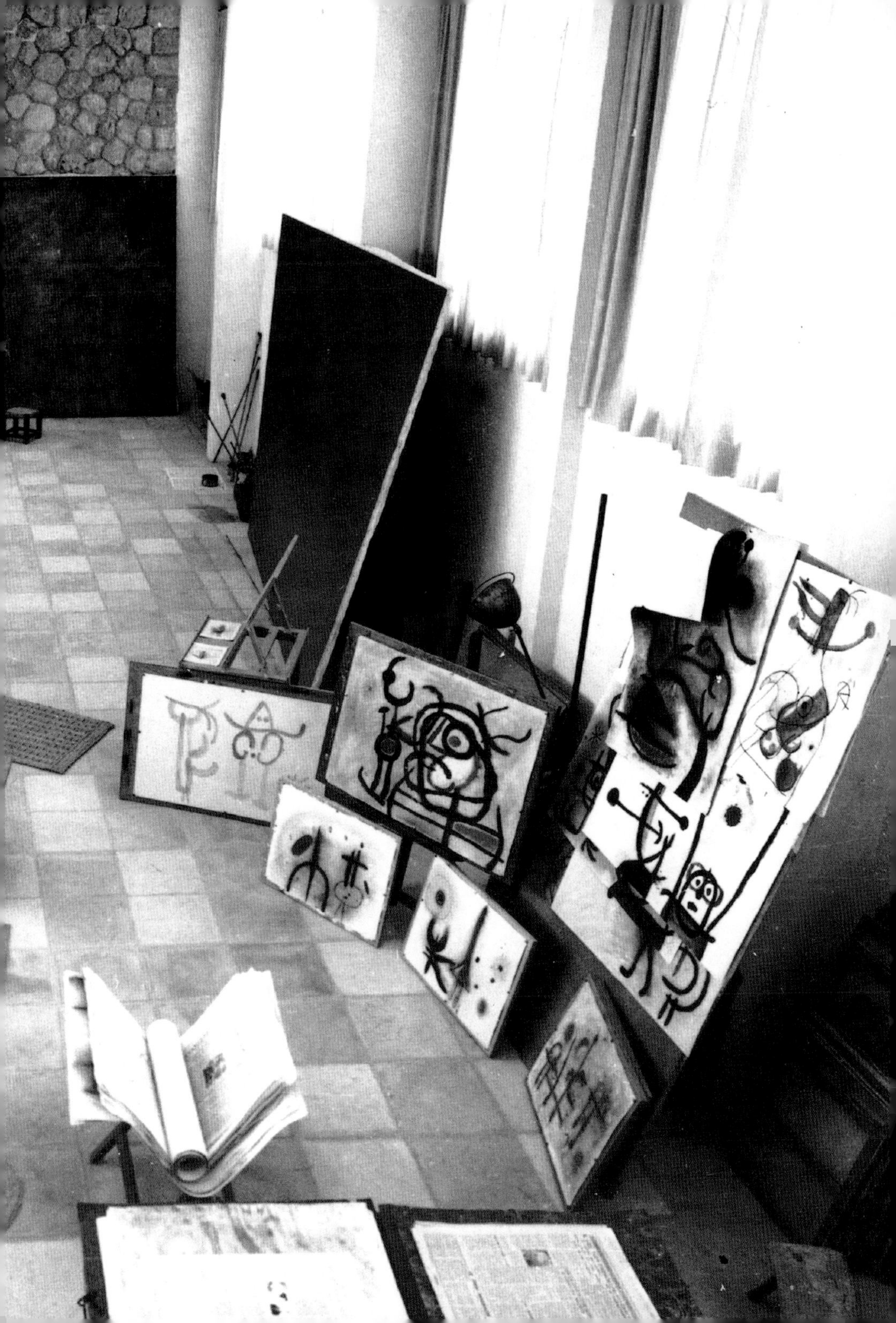

Produces a series of paintings on cardboard. He then stops painting until 1959 but continues working on ceramics and graphic arts.

1956

Sells the flat in Passatge del Crèdit and moves permanently to Palma, where he builds a house and commissions Josep Lluís Sert to design a studio for him.

1958

Inauguration of the two murals for UNESCO in Paris. The project receives the Guggenheim International Award.

1960

Works with Josep Llorens Artigas on the ceramic mural for Harkness Commons, Harvard University, to replace the mural painting.

1961

Publication of Jacques Dupin's book on Miró.

1962

Retrospective exhibition at the Musée National d'Art Moderne, Paris.

1964

Opening of the Fondation Maeght, designed by Josep Lluís Sert, and of the Labyrinth, with sculptures by Miró and Artigas, at Saint-Paul-de-Vence.

1966

Produces his first monumental sculptures in bronze, *Sun bird* and *Moon bird*.

Retrospective exhibition at the National Museum of Art, Tokyo.

Visits Japan for the first time, where he meets the poet Shuzo Takiguchi, author of the first monograph on Miró.

1967

Installation of a ceramic mural, produced in collaboration with Josep Llorens Artigas, at the Solomon R. Guggenheim Museum, New York.

Awarded the Carnegie International Grand Prize for painting.

1968

Last visit to the United States. Awarded an honorary doctorate by Harvard University.

Retrospective exhibitions at the Fondation Maeght, Saint-Paul-de-Vence, and at the Antic Hospital de la Santa Creu, Barcelona, sponsored by the City Council.

1969

"Miró otro" exhibition at the College of Architects, Barcelona. Miró paints the glass front of the building (an ephemeral action that is erased when the exhibition is over).

1970

Ceramic mural and mural painting for the Laughter Pavilion sponsored by Japanese gas companies at the Osaka World Fair.

In conjunction with Artigas, he produces a monumental ceramic mural for Barcelona Airport.

1972

The Fundació Joan Miró, Centre d'Estudis d'Art Contemporani, is legally constituted in Barcelona. Josep Lluís Sert is commissioned to design the building.

1975

The Fundació Joan Miró, Centre d'Estudis d'Art Contemporani, is opened to the public. A large selection of paintings, sculptures, textiles and prints are exhibited.

1976

Installation of the ceramic paving in the Pla de l'Os in the Rambla, Barcelona.

Official opening of the Fundació Joan Miró in Barcelona, with an exhibition of drawings from the collection donated by the artist.

Joan Miró working on the figures for the spectacle *Mori el Merma*, Sant Esteve de Palautordera (Barcelona), March 1977

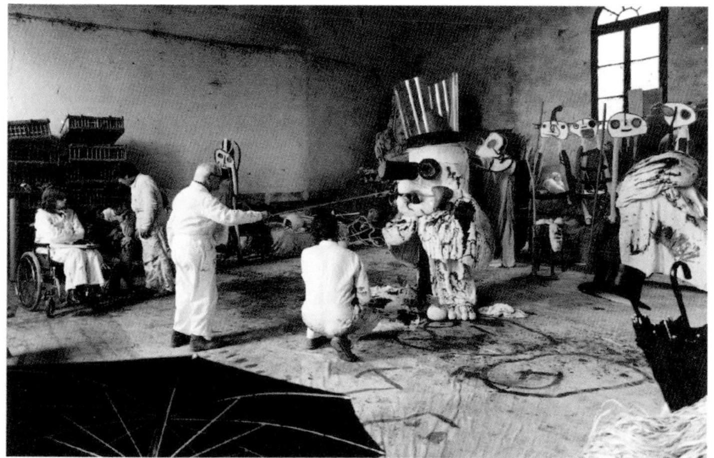

1977

Produces a large tapestry in conjunction with Josep Royo for the National Gallery, Washington D.C., and starts work on the tapestry for the Foundation.

Paints the sets and figures for *Mori el Merma* with the help of the actors in the Teatre de la Claca group.

1978

Retrospective exhibition at the Museo Español de Arte Contemporáneo, Madrid, organised in conjunction with the Fundació Joan Miró, Barcelona.

Premiere of *Mori el Merma* at the Gran Teatre del Liceu, Barcelona, performed by the Teatre de la Claca company, with giant puppets, masks and sets painted by Miró.

Unveiling of the monumental sculpture *Couple playing with almond blossom* in La Défense, Paris.

1979

Unveiling of the stained-glass windows at the Fondation Maeght, produced in collaboration with Charles Marcq, with whom Miró also made the stained-glass windows for the Chapelle Royale de Saint-Frambourg-de-Senlis, the venue for artistic and musical events held by the Cziffra Foundation.

Awarded an honorary doctorate by Barcelona University.

1980

King Juan Carlos awards him the Gold Medal for Fine Arts.

1981

Installation of the monumental sculpture known as *Miss Chicago* in Brunswick Plaza, Chicago.

1982

Installation of the monumental sculpture *Woman and bird* in the Parc de Joan Miró, Barcelona.

1983

Various events and exhibitions to celebrate Miró's ninetieth birthday.

"Joan Miró: A Ninetieth-Birthday Tribute" at the Museum of Modern Art, New York, and "Joan Miró: anys 20. Mutació de la realitat" at the Fundació Joan Miró, Barcelona.

Unveiling of a monumental sculpture in the courtyard of Barcelona City Hall.

Death of Joan Miró in Palma, Majorca, on 25 December. He is buried on 29 December in the Montjuïc cemetery, Barcelona.

Select Bibliography

1940

Takiguchi, Shûzo. *Miró,* Tokyo, Atelier.

1941

Sweeney, James Johnson. *Joan Miró,* New York, The Museum of Modern Art.

1947

Leiris, Michel. *The prints of Joan Miró,* New York, Curt Valentin.

1948

Greenberg, Clement. *Joan Miró,* New York, Quadrangle Press.

1949

Cirici, Alexandre. *Miró y la imaginación,* Barcelona, Omega.

Cirlot, Juan Eduardo. *Joan Miró,* Barcelona, Cobalto.

Queneau, Raymond. *Joan Miró ou le poète préhistorique,* Paris, Skira (Les trésors de la peinture française).

1954

Elgar, Frank. *Miró,* Paris, Fernand Hazan.

1956

Prévert, Jacques; Georges Ribemont-Dessaignes. *Joan Miró,* Paris, Maeght Éditeur.

Verdet, André; Roger Hauert. *Joan Miró,* Geneva, Kister.

1957

Duthuit, Georges. *Joan Miró,* Zurich, Ernst Scheidegger.

Hüttinger, Eduard. *Miró,* Berne, Alfred Scherz Verlag.

Scheidegger, Ernst. *Joan Miró: Gesammelte, Schriften, Fotos, Zeichnungen,* Zurich, Arche.

Verdet, André. *Joan Miró,* Nice, Galerie Matarasso.

1958

Baljeu, Joost. *Mondrian or Miró,* Amsterdam, De Beuk.

Hunter, Sam. *Joan Miró: His graphic work,* New York, Harry N. Abrams; *Joan Miró: L'œuvre gravé,* Paris, Calmann-Lévy; *Joan Miró: Das graphische Werk,* Stuttgart, Gerd Hatje; *Joan Miró: Su obra gráfica,* Barcelona, Gustavo Gili, 1959.

1959

Cela, Camilo José. *Joan Miró: Dibujos y litografías, Papeles de Son Armadans;* Barcelona, Seix y Barral; New York, New York Graphic Society.

Erben, Walter. *Joan Miró,* Munich, Prestel Verlag; London, Lund Humphries; Montecarlo, André Sauret; Mexico City, Hermes, 1961.

Soby, James Thrall. *Joan Miró*, New York, The Museum of Modern Art; Puerto Rico, Universidad de Río Piedras, 1960.
Sweeney, James Johnson. *Atmósfera Miró,* Barcelona, RM.
Wember, Paul. *Joan Miró farbige Lithographien*, Wiesbaden, Insel.
1960
Weelen, Guy. *Miró: 1924-1940*, Paris, Fernand Hazan; Barcelona, Gustavo Gili.
Weelen, Guy. *Miró: 1940-1955,* Paris, Fernand Hazan; Barcelona, Gustavo Gili.
1961
Borchert, Bernhard. *Joan Miró*, London, Faber and Faber.
Dupin, Jacques. *Miró*, Paris, Flammarion; New York, Harry N. Abrams; Cologne, Du Mont Schauberg; Milan, Mondadori, 1962.
1962
Taillandier, Yvon. *Creación Miró 1961,* Barcelona, RM.
1963
Gasch, Sebastià. *Joan Miró,* Barcelona, Alcides (Biografies populars).
Lassaigne, Jacques. *Miró,* Lausanne, Skira (Le goût de notre temps).
1964
Bonnefoy, Yves. *Miró,* Paris, Bibliothèque des Arts; Milan, Sylvana Editoriale d'Arte; New York, Viking Press, 1967; Barcelona, Juventud, 1970.
1965
Gasser, Manuel. *Joan Miró,* New York, Barnes & Noble; Paris, Marabout Université.
1966
Penrose, Roland. *Joan Miró: Creación en el espacio,* Barcelona, Polígrafa. Spanish, English, French and German editions.
1967
Dupin, Jacques. *Miró,* Paris, Union Générale d'Éditions (Collection d'Art Unesco 10/18, 380); Mexico City-Buenos Aires, Hermes; New York, Mentor Unesco Art Book.
Roditi, Edouard. *Chagall, Ernst, Miró,* Paris, Sedimo.
Walton, Paul H. *Dalí, Miró*, New York, Tudor.
1968
Bucci, Mario. *Joan Miró,* Florence, Sadea-Sansoni; Barcelona, Nauta, 1970.
1969
Greenberg, Clement. *Joan Miró*, New York, Arno Press.
1970
Cirici-Pellicer, Alexandre. *Miró en su obra,* Barcelona, Labor; Catalan edition: *Miró llegit,* Barcelona, Edicions 62, 1971.
Penrose, Roland. *Miró,* London, Thames & Hudson; Barcelona, Daimon, 1976; Catalan and Spanish edition: London, Thames and Hudson, and Barcelona, Destino, 1985; French edition: Paris, Thames and Hudson, 1990.
Perucho, Joan. *Joan Miró i Catalunya,* Barcelona, Polígrafa.
Sweeney, James Johnson. *Joan Miró,* Barcelona, Polígrafa.
Tapié, Michel. *Joan Miró*, Milan, Fratelli Fabbri; Paris, Hachette-Fabbri; Paris, Celiv, 1989.
1971
Chilo, Michel. *Miró: L'artiste et l'œuvre,* Paris, Maeght Editeur (Archives Maeght, 2).
Corredor-Matheos, José. *Miró,* Madrid, Dirección General de Bellas Artes.
Melià, Josep. *Joan Miró,* Barcelona, Dopesa.
Rowell, Margit. *Miró,* New York, Harry N. Abrams.

1972
Dupin, Jacques. *Miró escultor*, Barcelona, Polígrafa.
Herrmanns, Ralph. *Natten och drommen,* Stockholm, Bonnier; *La nit i el somni,* Barcelona, Sala Gaspar.
Hommage à Joan Miró, Paris, *XXe Siècle,* special issue.
Joan Miró, Milan, Artelevi.
Leiris, Michel; Fernand Mourlot. *Joan Miró lithographe I (1930-1952).* Paris, Maeght; Barcelona, Polígrafa; Geneva, Weber Éditeur.
Taillandier, Yvon. *Miró à l'encre,* Paris, *XXe Siècle; Mirografías*, Barcelona, Gustavo Gili.
Tono, Yoshiaki. *Ernst, Miró,* Tokyo, Shueisha.
1973
Jouffroy, Alain; Joan Teixidor. *Miró sculptures,* Paris, Maeght Éditeur (2nd extended edition: Paris, Maeght, 1980); *Miró plastik*, Munich, F. Bruckmann KG; *Miró Sculpture,* New York, Leon Amiel.
Rubin, William S. *Miró in the Collections of the Museum of Modern Art,* New York, The Museum of Modern Art.
1974
Diehl, Gaston. *Miró,* Paris, Flammarion.
Dopagne, Jacques. *Miró,* Paris, Fernand Hazan.
Herrmanns, Ralph. *Affischer av Miró 1937-1973,* Stockholm, AH Grafik.
Joan Miró, Paris, Éditions des Musées Nationaux.
Miró, Bilbao, La Gran Enciclopedia Vasca (Maestros actuales de la pintura y escultura catalanas, 22).
Pierre, José José Corredor-Matheos. *Céramiques de Miró et Artigas,* Paris, Maeght; *Miró & Artigas: Keramik*, Berne, Benteli.
1975
Fundació Joan Miró. *Fundació Joan Miró. Centre d'Estudis d'Art Contemporani.* Inaugural exhibition. June 1975, Barcelona, Fundació Joan Miró.
Permanyer, Lluís. *Los años difíciles de Miró, Llorens Artigas, Fenosa, Dalí, Clavé, Tàpies,* Barcelona, Lumen.
Queneau, Raymond. *Joan Miró lithographe II (1953-1963),* Paris, Maeght Éditeur; Barcelona, Polígrafa; Geneva, Weber.
1976
Picon, Gaëtan. *Joan Miró: Carnets Catalans,* Geneva, Albert Skira (Les sentiers de la création); *Joan Miró: Catalan Notebooks,* New York, Rizzoli, 1977; *Joan Miró: Carnets catalans,* Barcelona, Polígrafa, 1980; *Joan Miró: Cuadernos catalanes,* Barcelona, Polígrafa, 1980.
Rowell, Margit. *Joan Miró: Peinture-poésie*, Paris, Éditions de la Différence.
Teixidor, Joan. *Joan Miró lithographe III (1964-1969),* Paris, Maeght; Barcelona, Polígrafa, 1978.
1977
Cirici, Alexandre. *Miró-Mirall,* Barcelona, Polígrafa; *Miró et son temps,* Paris, Société Française du Livre.
Raillard, Georges. *Joan Miró: Ceci est la couleur de mes rêves,* Paris, Seuil; *Conversaciones con Joan Miró,* Barcelona, Granica, 1978; *I colori dei miei sogni: Conversazione con Georges Raillard*, Milan, Emme Edizioni, 1979.
1978
Gimferrer, Pere. Miró, *colpir sense nafrar,* Barcelona, Polígrafa; *Miró y su mundo,* Barcelona, Polígrafa; *Miró, catalan universel,* Hier et Demain.

Joan Miró, Madrid, Rayuela (Cuadernos Guadalimar ; 19).

Sabater, Gaspar. *Joan Miró y Mallorca,* Palma de Mallorca, Cort.

1980

Corredor-Matheos, José. *Los carteles de Miró,* Barcelona, Polígrafa; *Miró's Posters,* Secaucus, NJ, Chartwell Books; *Les affiches originales,* Paris, Cercle d'Art.

1981

Calas, Nicolás; Elena Calas. *Joan Miró lithographe IV (1969-1972),* Paris, Maeght; Barcelona, Polígrafa; Geneva, Weber Éditeur.

Franqui, Carlos; Jacques Dupin; Sylvano Bussotti. *Miró, l'Uccello Luce,* Venice, La Biennale.

Iscariotti, Patrizia. *Miró*, Rome, Armando Curcio (I classici della pintura).

Prévert, Jacques. *Couleurs de Braque, Calder, Miró,* Paris, Maeght Éditeur.

Román, József. *Miró,* Budapest, Corvina Kiadó.

1982

Schmalenbach, Werner. *Zeichnungen aus den späten Jahren,* Berlin, Propyläen.

1983

Malet, Rosa Maria. *Joan Miró,* Barcelona, Polígrafa, Catalan, Spanish and English editions; French edition: Paris, Albin Michel; German and Italian editions: Barcelona, Polígrafa, 1985.

Miró, Madrid, Sarpe (Los genios de la pintura española, 11).

Miró lithographs: 40 works by Joan Miró, New York, Dover Publications.

1984

Català-Roca, Francesc. *Miró noranta anys,* Barcelona, Edicions 62-Fundació Joan Miró.

Dupin, Jacques. *Miró graveur I (1928-1960),* Paris, Daniel Lelong, French, English and German editions; Spanish edition: Barcelona, Polígrafa, 1987.

Serra, Pere A. *Miró i Mallorca,* Barcelona, Polígrafa; Paris, Cercle d'Art; *Miró and Mallorca,* New York, Rizzoli, 1986.

Weelen, Guy. *Miró,* Paris, Nouvelles Éditions Françaises, 1984; Cologne, Du Mont Buchverlag; Milan, Garzanti.

1986

Rowell, Margit. *Joan Miró: Selected Writings and Interviews,* Boston, G.K. Hall; *Joan Miró: Écrits et entretiens,* Paris, Daniel Lelong, 1995.

1987

Jouffroy, Alain. *Miró,* Paris, Fernand Hazan.

1988

Erben, Walter. *Joan Miró 1893-1983: Mensch und Werk*, Cologne, Benedikt Taschen.

Obra de Joan Miró: Dibuixos, pintura, escultura, ceràmica, tèxtils, Barcelona, Fundació Joan Miró (Abridged edition: *La Fundació Joan Miró i les seves col·leccions,* Barcelona, Fundació Joan Miró, 1990. Catalan, Spanish, French and English editions).

1989

Cramer, Patrick. *Joan Miró: Catalogue raisonné des livres illustrés,* Geneva, Patrick Cramer; *Joan Miró: The illustrated books. Catalogue raisonné*, Geneva, Patrick Cramer.

Dupin, Jacques. *Miró graveur II (1961-1973),* Paris, Daniel Lelong, French, English and German editions; Spanish edition: Barcelona, Polígrafa.

Raillard, Georges. *Miró,* Paris, Hazan (Les chefs d'œuvre); Spanish edition: Madrid, Debate, 1993 (Grandes maestros de la Pintura moderna).

1990

Combalía, Victoria. *El descubrimiento de Miró: Miró y sus críticos, 1918-1929,* Barcelona, Destino.

Joan Miró, Paris, Éditions des Musées Nationaux, Grand Palais.

Sert, Josep Lluís. *Taller per a Joan Miró,* Palma de Mallorca, Col·legi Oficial d'Arquitectes.

1991

Bernier, Rosamond. *Matisse, Picasso, Miró as I knew them,* New York, Alfred A. Knopf.

Dupin, Jacques. *Miró graveur III (1973-1975),* Paris, Daniel Lelong, French, English and German editions; Spanish edition: Barcelona, Polígrafa.

Green, Christopher. *Picasso y Miró, 1930: El mago, el niño y el artista,* Valencia, IVAM-Generalitat Valenciana.

Green, Christopher; Hilton Kramer. *Joan Miró i la mort de la pintura: Dos excursos,* Barcelona, Barcanova.

1992

Cramer, Patrick. *Joan Miró lithographe V (1972-1975),* Paris, Maeght Éditeur. French, English and Spanish editions.

Fernández Miró, David. *David: Escritos de David Fernández Miró,* Barcelona, Fundació Joan Miró, Edicions 62; Palma de Mallorca, Fundació Pilar i Joan Miró.

Malet, Rosa Maria. *Joan Miró,* Barcelona, Edicions 62 (Col·lecció Pere Vergés de Biografies, 47).

Prete, Cecilia. *Miró,* Milan, Electa. Spanish edition: Madrid, Sociedad Editorial Electa España, 1995.

1993

Corbella, Domènec. *Entendre Miró: Anàlisi del llenguatge mironià a partir de la "Sèrie Barcelona" 1939-1944,* Barcelona, Publicacions de la Universitat de Barcelona.

Dupin, Jacques. *Joan Miró,* Barcelona, Polígrafa, Catalan, Spanish and English editions; French edition: Paris, Flammarion.

Gimferrer, Pere. *Les arrels de Miró,* Barcelona, Polígrafa; *Las raices de Miró,* Barcelona, Polígrafa; *The roots of Miró,* New York, Rizzoli; *Joan Miró: Auf den Spuren seiner Kunst,* Stuttgart, Daco-Verlag-Günter-Bläse.

Saura, Antonio. *Belvédère Miró,* Paris, L'Échoppe.

Scheidegger, Ernst. *Joan Miró a Catalunya: Huellas de un encuentro,* Paris, Maeght. Also French and English editions. German edition: Zurich, Ernst Scheidegger.

1994

Gassner, Hubertus. *Joan Miró: Der magische Gartner,* Cologne, Dumont.

Giralt-Miracle, Daniel. *El crit de la terra: Joan Miró i el Camp de Tarragona,* Barcelona, Columna (Tamarit, 4).

Santos Torroella, Rafael. *35 años de Joan Miró,* Barcelona, Parsifal Ediciones (Figuras, 30).

1995

Catoir, Barbara. *Miró on Mallorca,* Munich-New York, Prestel; *Miró auf Mallorca,* Munich-New York, Prestel.

Miró grabador en los fondos del Museo Nacional Centro de Arte Reina Sofía, Madrid, Museo Nacional Centro de Arte Reina Sofía.

1996

Punyet Miró, Joan. *Miró: L'Atelier*, Paris, Éditions Assouline; *Miró in his Studio,* London, Thames and Hudson.

Schildkraut, Joseph J.; Aurora Otero (eds.). *Depression and the Spiritual in Modern Art: Homage to Miró*, Chichester, etc., John Wiley & Sons.

1998

Combalía, Victoria. *Picasso-Miró: Miradas cruzadas,* Madrid, Electa.

Photographs

Raoul Barba: page 111
Neus D. Calvet: page 19
Colita: page 16
Daniel Font: page 14
F. Català Roca: pages 6, 16, 18, 101, 102, 113, 114-115, 117
Ferran Freixa: page 9
Joaquim Gomis: pages 8, 112
Joaquim Jansana and Montse Pastor: pages 9, 12
Man Ray: page 106
Pere Pratdesaba: pages 13, 20
Serra, Arxiu Històric de la Ciutat (Barcelona): page 108
Successió Miró: pages 107, 108

Board of Trustees of the Joan Miró Foundation